PLANTATION

EDITION

VOLUME XII

Thomas Nelson Page.

❧ THE NOVELS, STORIES, SKETCHES AND POEMS OF THOMAS NELSON PAGE ❧

THE OLD SOUTH
ESSAYS SOCIAL AND POLITICAL

CHARLES SCRIBNER'S SONS
NEW YORK, ❧ ❧ ❧ ❧ 1906

TO

MY COUNTRYMEN

AND

COUNTRYWOMEN

PREFACE

Several of the within essays were delivered as addresses before literary Alumni Societies, and revision has not wholly availed to clear them from the rhetoric which insensibly crept into them. Being, however, upon topics as to which there is much diversity of sentiment, this form of expression will at least serve to show the state of feeling where they were delivered and thus may not be without its use. The substance of the papers is what the author earnestly believes and what he is satisfied history will establish.

The essays are given to the public in the hope that they may serve to help awaken inquiry into the true history of the Southern people and may aid in dispelling the misapprehension under which the Old South has lain so long.

CONTENTS

ILLUSTRATIONS

THE OLD SOUTH

THE OLD SOUTH

IN the selection of a theme for this occasion, I have, curious to relate, been somewhat embarrassed. Not that good subjects were not manifold, and material plentiful; but for me, on this occasion, when I am to address this audience, in this presence, there could be but one subject—the best.

I deem myself fortunate that I am permitted to address you on this spot; for this University, whose friend was George Washington and whose establisher was Robert E. Lee, impresses me as the spot on earth to which my discourse is most appropriate. Broad enough to realize the magnificent ideal of its first benefactor as a university where the youth of this whole country may meet and acquire the grand idea of this American Union, it is yet so distinctly free from the materialistic tendencies which of late are assailing kindred institutions and insidiously threatening even the existence of the Union itself, that it may be justly regarded as the citadel of that conservatism which, mated with immortal devotion to duty, may be termed the cardinal doctrine of the Southern civilization.

Something more than twenty years ago there fell upon the South a blow for which there is no parallel among the casualties which may happen to an individual, and which has rarely in history befallen nations. Under the euphemism of reconstruction an attempt was made after the war to destroy the South. She was dismembered, disfranchised, denationalized. The States which composed her were turned by her conquerors into military districts, and their governments were subverted to military tribunals. Virginia, that had given Washington, Jefferson, Henry, Nelson, the Lees, Madison, Marshall, and a host of others who had made the nation, became "District No. 1."

The South was believed to be no more. It was intended that she should be no more. But God in his providence had his great purpose for her and He called her forth. With the old spirit strong within her she renewed her youth like the eagles, fixed her gaze upon the sun, and once more spreading her strong pinions, lifted herself for another flight.

The outside world gazed astonished at her course, and said, this is not the Old South, but a new civilization, a New South.

The phrase by imperative inference institutes invidious comparison with and implies censure of something else—of some other order—of a different civilization.

That order, that civilization, I propose to discuss briefly this evening; to, so far as may be in the narrow limits of an address, repel this censure; show that comparison is absurd, and that the New South is, in fact, simply the Old South with its energies directed into new lines.

The civilization which is known by this name was as unique as it was distinct. It combined elements of the three great civilizations which since the dawn of history have enlightened the world. It partook of the philosophic tone of the Grecian, of the dominant spirit of the Roman, and of the guardfulness of individual rights of the Saxon civilization. And over all brooded a softness and beauty, the joint product of Chivalry and Christianity.

This individuality began almost with the

5

first permanent Anglo-Saxon settlement of this continent; for the existence of its distinguishing characteristics may be traced from the very beginning of the colonial period. The civilization flourished for two hundred and fifty years, and until its vitality, after four years of invasion and war, expired in the convulsive throes of reconstruction.

Its distinctiveness, like others of its characteristics, was referable to its origin, and to its subsequent environing conditions.

Its tendency was towards exclusiveness and conservatism. It tolerated no invasion of its rights. It admitted the jurisdiction of no other tribunal than itself. The result was not unnatural. The world, barred out, took its revenge, and the Old South stands to-day charged with sterility, with attempting to perpetuate human slavery, and with rebellion.

That there was shortcoming in certain directions may not be denied; but it was not what is charged.

If, when judged by the narrow standard of mere, common materialism, the Southern civilization fell short, yet there is another standard by which it measured the fullest stature: the sudden supremacy of the American people to-day is largely due to the Old South, and to its contemned civilization.

The difference between the Southern civilization and the Northern was the result of the difference between their origins and subsequent surroundings.

The Northern colonies of Great Britain in America were the asylums of religious zealots and revolutionists who at their first coming were bent less on the enlargement of their fortunes than on the freedom to exercise their religious convictions, however much the sudden transition from dependence and restriction to freedom and license may in a brief time have tempered their views of liberty and changed them into proscriptors of the most tyrannical type.

The Southern colonies, on the other hand, were from the first the product simply of a desire for adventure, for conquest, and for wealth.

The Northern settlements were, it is true, founded under the law; but it was well understood that they contained an element which was not friendly to the government and that the latter was well satisfied to have the seas stretch between them. The Southern, on the other hand, came with the consent of the crown, the blessing of the Church, and under the auspices and favor of men of high standing in the kingdom. They came with all the ceremonial of an elaborate civil government—with an executive, a council deputed by authorities at home, and formal and minute instructions and regulations.

The crown hoped to annex the unknown land lying between the El Dorado, which Spain had obtained amid the summer seas, and the unbounded claims of its hereditary enemy, France, to the North and West.

The Church, which viewed the independence of the Northern refugees as schism, if not heresy, gave to this enterprise its benison in the belief that "the adventurers for the plantations of Virginia were the most noble and worthy advancers of the standard of Christ among the Gentiles." The company organized and equipped successive expeditions in the hope of gain; and soldiers of fortune, and gentlemen in misfortune, threw in their lot in the certainty of adventure and the probability that they might better their condition.

Under such auspices the Southern colonies necessarily were rooted in the faith of the England from which they came—political, religious, and civil. Thus from the very beginning the spirit of the two sections was absolutely different, and their surrounding conditions were for a long time such as to keep them diverse.

The first governor of the colony of Virginia was a member of a gentle Huntingdonshire family, and he was succeeded in office by a long line of men, most of them of high degree. In the first ship-load of colonists there were "four carpenters, twelve laborers, and fifty-four gentlemen."

John Smith, the strongest soul that planted the British spirit upon this continent, and who was himself a soldier of fortune, cried out in the bitterness of his heart against such colonists; yet he came afterwards to note that these "gentlemen" cut down more trees in a day than the ordinary laborers.

With the controversy as to whether or not the inhabitants of the Southern colonies were generally the descendants of Cavaliers it is not necessary to deal. It makes no difference now to the race which established this Union whether its ancestors fought with the Norman conqueror on Senlac Hill or whether they were among the "villains" who followed the standards of Harold's earls. It may, however, be averred that the gentle blood and high connection which undoubtedly existed in a considerable degree exerted widely a strengthening and refining power, and were potent in their influence to elevate and sustain not only the families which claimed to be their immediate possessors, but through them the entire colonial body, social and politic.

I make a prouder claim than this: the inhabitants of these colonies were the strongest strains of many stocks—Saxon, Celt, and Teuton; Cavalier and Puritan.

The ship-loads of artisans and adventurers who came, caught in time the general spirit, and found in the new country possibilities never dreamed of in the old. Each man, whether gentle or simple, was compelled to assert himself in the land where personal force was of more worth than family position, however exalted; but having proved his personal title to individual respect, he was eager to approve likewise his claim to honorable lineage, which still was held at high value. The royal governors, with all the accompaniments of a vice-regal court, only so much modified as was necessary to suit the surroundings, kept before the people the similitude of royal state; and generation after generation of large planters and thriving merchants, with broad grants acquired from the crown or by their own enterprise, as they rose, fell into the tendency of the age and perpetuated or augmented the spirit of the preceding generation.

With the Huguenot immigration came a new accession of the same spirit, intensified in some directions, if tempered in others.

As society grew more and more indulgent its demands became greater; the comforts of life became more readily obtainable in the colonies just at the time that civil and religious restrictions became more burdensome in the old country, and the stream of immigration began to flow more freely.

Slavery had become meantime a factor in the problem—potent at first for perhaps mitigated good, finally for immeasurable ill to all except the slaves themselves.

This class of labor was so perfectly suited to the low alluvial lands of the tide-water section that each generation found itself wealthier than that which had preceded it, and it was evident that the limits between the mountains and the coast would soon be too narrow for a

race which had colonized under a charter that
ran "up into the land to the farthest sea."

To this reason was added that thirst for adventure and that desire for glory which is a
characteristic of the people, and in Virginia
Spottswood and his Knights of the Golden
Horseshoe set out to ride to the top of the Blue
Ridge, which till then was the barricade beyond
which no Saxon was known to have ventured,
and from which it was supposed the Great
Lakes might be visible. They found not "the
unsalted seas," but one of the fairest valleys
on earth stretched before them; and the Old
Dominion suddenly expanded from a narrow
province to a land from whose fecund womb
commonwealths and peoples have sprung.

By a strange destiny, almost immediately
succeeding this discovery, the vitality of the
colony received an infusion of another element,
which became in the sequel a strong part of
that life which in its development made the
"Southern civilization."

This element occupied the new valley and
changed it from a hunting-ground to a garden. The first settler, it is said, came to it
by an instinct as imperative as that which
brought the dove back to the ark of safety.

It was not the dove, however, which came when John Lewis settled in this valley; but an eagle, and in his eyry he reared a brood of young who have been ever ready to strike for the South. He had been forced to leave Ireland because he had slain his landlord, who was attempting to illegally evict him, and the curious epitaph on his tomb begins, "Here lies John Lewis, who slew the Irish Lord."

He was followed by the McDowells, Alexanders, Prestons, Grahams, Reids, McLaughlins, Moores, Wallaces, McCluers, Mathews, Woods, Campbells, Waddells, Greenlees, Bowyers, Andersons, Breckenridges, Paxtons, Houstons, Stuarts, Gambles, McCorkles, Wilsons, McNutts, and many others, whose descendants have held the highest offices in the land which their fortitude created, and who have ever thrown on the side of principle the courage, resolution, and loyalty with which they held out for liberty and Protestantism in the land from which they came.

It was a sturdy strain which had suddenly flung itself along the frontier, and its effect has been plainly discernible in the subsequent history of the Old South, running a somewhat sombre thread in the woof of its civilization, but giving it "a body" which perhaps it might otherwise not have possessed. A somewhat similar element, though springing from a different source, held the frontier in the other States. Its force was not towards the East, but towards the West; not towards the sea and the old country, but towards the mountains and the new; and to its energy was due the Western settlement, as to the other and the older class was due the Eastern.

As the latter had created and opened up the first tier of States along the sea-coast, so these newcomers now crossed the mountains, penetrated "the dark and bloody ground," and conquered the second tier, hewing out of primeval forests—and holding them alike against Indians, French and British—the States of Ohio, Kentucky, and Tennessee, and opening up for the first time the possibility of a great American continent.

They were not slave-holders to a great extent; for they were frontiersmen, who mainly performed their own work; they were not generally connected with the old families of the Piedmont and Tidewater, for they had in large part entered the State by her northern boundary, or had been brought to take up land under "cabin rights," or had come across the mountain barrier and had cut their own way into the forests, and they traced their lineage to Caledonian stock; they were not bound to them by the ties of a common religion, for they repudiated the Anglican Church, with its hierarchy and "malignant doctrines," as that Church had repudiated them, and they worshipped God, according to their own consciences, "in a way agreable to the principles of their education."

Thus, neither by interest, blood, nor religion, were they for a time connected with the original settlers of the Southern colonies; and yet they were distinctly and irrevocably an integral part of the South and of the Southern civilization,—as the waters of the Missouri and the upper Mississippi are said to flow side by side for a hundred miles, each distinguishable, yet both together mingling to make the majestic Father of Waters.

There was something potent in the Southern soil, which drew to it all who once rested on its bosom, without reference to race, or class, or station. Let men but once breathe the air of the South and generally they were thenceforth Southerners forever. So, having crossed the mountains, this race made Kentucky and Tennessee Southern States, and, against the allurements of their own interest and the appeals of the North, held them so, and infused a strong Southern element into the State of Ohio.

Steam had not been then invented, and the infinite forces of electricity were as yet unknown; yet, without these two great civilizers, the Southern spirit bore the ensign of the Anglo-Saxon across the mountains, seized the West, and created this American continent.

There is another work which the South may justly claim. As it pushed advance up first against the French confines and then beyond them, and made this country English, so it preserved the spirit of civil and religious liberty pure and undefiled, and established it as the guiding star of the American people forever.

I believe that the subordination of everything else to this principle is the key to the Southern character.

The first charter of Virginia, the leading Southern colony, "secured" to her people "the privileges, franchises, and immunities of native-born Englishmen forever," and they never forgot it nor permitted others to over-look it.

She had a Legislative Assembly as early as 1619, and the records show that it guarded with watchful vigilance against all encroach-ments those rights which, thanks to it, are to-day regarded as inalienable among all Eng-lish-speaking races.

The assembly was hardly established be-fore it struck its first blow for constitutional liberty.

When the royal commissioners sent by James to investigate the ''Seditious Parlia-ment'' came and demanded the records of the Assembly it refused to give them up; and when the clerk, under a bribe, surrendered them, the Assembly stood him in the pillory and cut off one of his ears. This did not save their charter; but in the sequel it turned out that the forfeiture of the charter was a great blessing.

As early as 1623-24 the General Assembly of the colony adopted resolutions defining and declaring the right of the colonists, and limiting the powers of the executive.

The governor was not ''to lay any taxes or impositions upon the colony, their lands, or other way than by authority of the General Assembly, to be levied and employed as the General Assembly shall appoint.'' Moreover, the governor was not to withdraw the inhabitants from their labor for his service, and the Burgesses attending the General Assembly were to be privileged from arrest.

The colony of Maryland went farthest yet in the way of liberty, and, under the direction of Lord Baltimore, passed the famous Act of Toleration on the 2d of April, 1649, which first established the principle of freedom of conscience on the earth.

Thus early was the South striking for those great principles of liberty which are fundamental now mainly because of the spirit of our forefathers. It was not until some years after Virginia had declared herself that the issue was finally joined in England.

From this time the light of liberty flamed like a beacon. The colonies declared themselves devotedly loyal to the crown, but were more true to their own rights; and they frequently found themselves opposed to the government as vested in and manifested by the royal governor.

During the time of the Commonwealth the

Southern colonies held by the crown, and became the asylum of many hard-pressed Cavaliers who found Cromwell's interest in them too urgent to permit them to remain at home. And Charles II himself was offered a crown by his loyal subjects in Virginia when he was a fugitive with a price set on his head.

So notorious was this fealty that the Great Protector was obliged to send a war fleet to Virginia to quell this spirit and to make terms of peace. The treaty is made as between independent powers.

The colonies were to obey the Commonwealth; but this submission was to be acknowledged a voluntary act, not forced nor constrained by a conquest upon the country. The people were "to enjoy such freedom and privileges as belong to free-born people in England." The continuance of their Representative Assembly was guaranteed. There was to be total indemnity. The colony was to have free trade, notwithstanding the Navigation Act. The General Assembly alone was to have the power to levy taxes; and there were other provisions securing those privileges and immunities which were claimed as the birthright of the race.

After Cromwell's death the General Assembly declared the supreme power to be "resident in" itself until such command or commission should come out of England as the General Assembly adjudged lawful. And when the king once more came into his own the General Assembly accepted his governor willingly, as did the colony of Maryland, but held firmly to the advantages it had secured during the interregnum.

The colony welcomed the followers of Cromwell in the hour of their adversity, and offered them as secure an asylum as it had done a few years before to the hard-pressed Cavaliers. Thus society came to be knit of the strongest elements of all parties and classes, who merged all factions into loyalty for their collective rights.

Then came the contest with Berkeley. Charles forgot the people who offered him a kingdom when he was an exile and a wanderer, and his representative neglected their rights.

England claimed the monopoly of the colonial trade, and imposed a heavy duty on their exports. Not content with this, the silly king gave away half of the settled portion of Virginia to two of his followers. The colony sent commissioners to protest, but before the trouble could be remedied Virginia, demanding self-government, flamed into revolution, with Nathaniel Bacon at its head.

We are told that the great revolution of 1688 established the liberties of the English people. The chief Southern colony of Great Britain had fought out its revolution twelve years before, and although the revolution failed disastrously for its participants, and it has come down in history as a rebellion, yet its ends were gained.

The troops of the fiery Bacon were beaten and scattered, those who were captured were hanged as insurrectionists, and the gallant leader himself died of fever contracted in the trenches, a fugitive and an outlaw, with a stigma so welded to his name that after two centuries he is known but as "Bacon the Rebel."

Judged by the narrow standard which makes success the sole test, Nathaniel Bacon was a rebel, and the uprising which he headed was a rebellion; but there are "rebellions" which are not rebellions, but great revolutions, and there are "rebels" who, however absolutely their immediate purposes may have failed, and

21

however unjustly contemporary history may have recorded their actions, shall yet be known to posterity as patriots pure and lofty, whose motives and deeds shall evoke the admiration of all succeeding time.

Such was Nathaniel Bacon. They called him rebel and outlawed him; but he headed a revolution for the protection of the same rights, the same "privileges, franchises, and immunities," whose infringement caused another revolution just one hundred years later, the leader of whose armies was the rebel George Washington, the founder of this University.

The elder rebel failed of his purpose for the time, yet haply but for that stalwart blow struck at Jamestown for the rights of the colonists there had never been a Declaration of Independence, a Bunker Hill, a Yorktown, or the United States of America.

The spirit never receded. The opening up of lands, the increase of slaves, the extension of commerce, made the Southern colonies wealthier generation after generation, and their population filled the territory up to the mountains and then flowed over, as we have seen, into the unknown regions beyond; and generation after generation, as they grew stronger, they grew more self-contained, more independent, more assertive of their rights, more repellant of any invasion, more jealous of tyranny, more loving of liberty.

Against governors, councils, metropolitans, commissaries, and clergy, in the Burgesses and in the vestries, they fought the fight with steadfast courage and persistency.

The long contest between the vestries and the Church was only a different phase of this same spirit, and was in reality the same struggle between the colony and the government at home, transferred to a different theatre. The planters were churchmen; but they claimed the right to control the Church, and repudiated the right of the Church to control them. It was the sacred right of self-government for which they contended; and the first cry of "treason" was when the contest culminated in that celebrated Parsons case, in which the orator of the Revolution burst suddenly into fame.

"The gentleman has spoken treason," declared the counsel for the plaintiff; but it was the treason that was in all hearts, and was the first step of the young advocate in his ascent to a fame for oratory so transcending that the mind of a later and more prosaic generation fails to grasp its wondrousness, and there is nothing by which to measure it since the day when the Athenian orator thundered against the Macedonian tyrant.

The same principles which inspired the uprising of Bacon a century before, and had animated the continuous struggle since, swept the colonies into revolution now.

The Stamp Act of 1766 set the colonies into flame, and from this time to the outbreak of flagrant war, a decade later, the people stood with steadfast faces set against all encroachment; and when the time came for war the South sprang to arms. She did not enter upon the enterprise from ignorance of her danger, nor yet in recklessness.

The Southern planter sent his son to England to be educated, and many of the men who sat in the great conventions, or who subscribed the Declaration of Independence, had been themselves educated in England, and knew full well the magnitude of the hazard they were assuming in instituting with a handful of straggling colonies a revolution against a power which made Chatham the ruler of Europe, and which only a generation later tore the victorious eagles of Napoleon himself.

Thomas Nelson, Jr., the wealthiest man in the Colony of Virginia, had sat by Charles James Fox at Eton and knew England and her power. Others did also.

They knew all this full well; and yet for the sake of those principles, of those rights and liberties, which they believed were theirs of right, and which they meant to transmit undiminished to their children, they gave up wealth and ease and security, blazoned on their standard the motto "Virginia for Constitutional Liberty," and launched undaunted on the sea of revolution.

There is an incident connected with the signing of the Declaration of Independence, which illustrates at once the character of the Southern planter and the point I am endeavoring to make.

You may have observed, in looking over the signers of the Declaration of Independence, that Charles Carroll of Maryland subscribed himself "Charles Carroll of Carrollton." Unless you know the story it would appear that simple arrogance prompted such a subscription. The facts, however, were these: It was a serious occasion, and a solemn act this group of men were performing, assembled to affix their names to this document, which was to be forever a barrier between them and Great Britain; it had not been so very long since the headsman's axe had fallen for a less overt treason than they were then publicly declaring, and if they failed they were likely to feel its weight or else to meet a yet more disgraceful death.

Benjamin Franklin had just replied to the remark, "We must all hang together," with his famous pleasantry, "Yes, or we shall all hang separately," when Carroll, perhaps the wealthiest man in Maryland, took the pen. As he signed his name, Charles Carroll," and rose from his seat, some one said, "Carroll, you will get off easily; there are so many Charles Carrolls they will never know which one it is." Carroll walked back to the table, and, seizing the pen again, stooped and wrote under his name "of Carrollton."

They affixed their names to the Declaration, comprehending the peril they were braving, as well as they did the propositions which they were enunciating to the world, and they intended to shoulder all the responsibility of their act.

The South emerged from the Revolution mangled and torn, but free, and with the Anglo-Saxon spirit whetted by success and intensified.

She emerged also with her character already established, and with those qualities permanently fixed which subsequently came to be known through their results as the Southern civilization.

Succeeding the Revolution came a period not very distinctly marked in the common idea of important steps, but full of hazard and equally replete with pregnant results—a period in which the loose and impotent Confederation became through the patriotism of the South this Union.

At last, the Constitution was somewhat of a compromise, and the powers not expressly delegated to Congress were reserved to each State in her sovereign capacity, and it was upon this basis simply that the Union was established.

It may throw light on the part that the South took in this to recall the fact that when the point was made that Virginia should relinquish her Northwestern territory, Virginia ceded to the country, without reservation, the territory stretching north to the Great Lakes and west to the Father of Waters. She granted it without consideration, and without grudging, as she had always given generously whenever she was called upon, and when she had stripped herself

27

of her fairest domain, in retribution a third of the small part which she had retained was torn from her, without giving her even a voice to protest against it. There is no act of the Civil War, or of its offspring, the days of reconstruction, so arbitrary, so tyrannical, and so unjustifiable.

When the South emerged from the Revolutionary War, her character was definitely recognized as manifesting the qualities which combined to give her civilization the peculiar and strongly marked traits that have made it since distinctive among the English-speaking races. And in the succeeding years these traits became more and more prominent.

The guiding principle of the South had steadily been what may be termed public spirit; devotion to the rights and liberties of the citizen, the embodiment of which in a form of government was aptly termed the Commonwealth.

To this yielded even the aristocratic sentiment. The Southerner was attached to the British mode of inheritance, yet he did away with the law of primogeniture; he was devoted to the traditions of his Church, yet he declared for religious freedom, and not only disestablished the Church, but confiscated and made common the Church lands, and it is due to the South, to-day, that man is free to worship God according to his conscience wherever the true God is known and feared.

The South changed far less after its separation from Great Britain than did the North. Indeed, the change was during the entire *antebellum* period comparatively small when viewed beside the change in the other portion of the country.

It has been said that it was provincial. It certainly did not so consider itself, for it held a self-esteem and self-content as unquestioning and sublime as that which pervaded Rome; and wherever the provinces were, they were to the Southerner assuredly beyond the confines of the Southern States. Yet the naked fact is, that, assuming provincialism to be what it has been aptly defined to be, "localism, or being on one side and apart from the general movement of contemporary life," the South was provincial.

African slavery, which had proven ill-adapted to the needs and conditions of the North, and consequently had disappeared more because of this fact than because of the efforts of the Abolitionists, had proven perfectly suited to the needs of the South.

The negro flourished under the warm skies of the South, and the granaries and tobacco fields of Maryland and Virginia, the cotton-fields of the Carolinas, Georgia, and Alabama, and the sugar plantations of the Mississippi States, bore ample testimony to his utility as a laborer. But the world was moving with quicker strides than the Southern planter knew, and slavery was banishing from his land all the elements of that life which was keeping stride with progress without. Thus, before the Southerner knew it, the temper of the time had changed, slavery was become a horror, and he himself was left behind and was in the opposition.

Changes came, but they did not affect the South —it remained as before or changed in less ratio; progress was made; the rest of the world fell into the universal movement; but the South advanced more slowly. It held by its old tenets when they were no longer tenable, by its ancient customs when, perhaps, they were no longer defensible. All interference from the outside was repelled as officious and inimical, and all intervention was instantly met with hostility and indignation. It believed itself the home of liberality when it was, in fact, necessarily

30

intolerant;—of enlightenment, of progress, when it had been so far distanced that it knew not that the world had passed by.

The cause of this was African slavery, with which the South is taunted as if she alone had instituted it. For this she suffered; for this, at last, she was forced to fight and pour out her blood like water.

Slavery had forced the South into a position where she must fight or surrender her rights.

The fight on the part of the North was for the power to adapt the Constitution to its new doctrine, and yet to maintain the Union; on the part of the South, it was for the preservation of guaranteed constitutional rights.

Through the force of circumstances and under "an inexorable political necessity," the South found itself compelled to assume finally the defence of the system; but it was not responsible either for its origin or its continuance, and the very men who fought to prevent external interference with it had spent their lives endeavoring to solve the problem of its proper abolition.

The African slave trade, dating from about the year 1442 (although it did not flourish for a century or more), when it was begun by Anthony Gonzales, a Portuguese, was continued until the present century was well installed.

It was chartered and encouraged by Queen Elizabeth, and by her royal successors, against the protest of the Southern colonies, down to the time of the American Revolution. The first nation on the civilized globe to protest against it as monstrous was the Southern colony, Virginia. Twenty-three times her people protested to the crown in public acts of her Assembly.

One of the most scathing charges, brought by the writer of the Declaration of Independence against the crown, was that in which he arraigns the king of England for having "waged cruel war against human nature itself, violating its most sacred rights of life and liberty in the persons of a distant people who never offended him, captivating and carrying them into slavery in another hemisphere, or incurring a miserable death in their transportation thither.

"This piratical warfare, the opprobrium of infidel powers, is the warfare of the Christian king of Great Britain.

"Determined to keep open a market where men should be bought and sold, he has prostituted his negative for suppressing any legislative attempt to prohibit and restrain the execrable commerce," etc.

This clause was the product of Thomas Jefferson, a Southerner, and although it was stricken out in compliance with the wishes of two of the Southern colonies, yet substantially the same charge was made in the Constitution of Virginia, where in its preamble is set forth "the detestable and insupportable tyranny of the king of Great Britain, that he had prompted to rise in rebellion those very negroes whom by any inhuman use of his royal negative he had refused us permission to exclude by law."

If the South had at any previous time inclined to profit by the slave trade, it was only in common with the rest of Christendom—particularly with New England—when the most zealous and religious were participants in it; when the Duke of York, the future sovereign himself, was the head of the company chartered under the Great Seal of England, and when the queen-mother, the queen-consort, Prince Rupert, the Earl of Shaftesbury, and the leading men of the times were incorporators.

Even the godly John Newton was interested in the traffic.

In the South, however, long before Jefferson framed his famous arraignment of the king of Great Britain, protest on protest had been made against the iniquity, and all the ingenuity of those men who produced the Declaration of Independence and the Constitution of the United States had been exercised to bring it to an end

The House of Burgesses often attempted to lay a duty of from £10 to £20 a head on the negro slaves, and against the veto of the crown they continued to levy duties, until the oppression by the crown culminated, and "The gentlemen of the House of Burgesses and the body of merchants assembled in the old capital of Virginia on the 2d June, 1770, resolved, among other things, that we will not import or bring into the colony, or cause to be imported or brought into the colony, either by sea or land, any slaves, or make sale of any upon commission, or purchase any slave or slaves that may be imported by others, after the 1st day of November next, unless the same have been twelve months on the continent."

On the 1st of April, 1772, the House of Burgesses addressed a hot petition to the crown, "imploring his Majesty's paternal assistance in averting a calamity of a most alarming nature.'' It proceeds: ''The importation of slaves into the colonies from the coast of Africa hath long been considered as a trade of great inhumanity, and under its present encouragement we have too much reason to fear will endanger the very existence of your Majesty's American dominions. We are sensible that some of your Majesty's subjects of Great Britain may reap emoluments from this sort of traffic, but when we consider that it greatly retards the settlement of the colonies with more useful inhabitants, and may in time have the most destructive influence, we presume to hope that the interest of a few will be disregarded when placed in competition with the security and happiness of such numbers of your Majesty's dutiful and loyal servants. Deeply impressed with these sentiments, we most humbly beseech your Majesty to remove all those restraints on your Majesty's governors of the colony which inhibit their assenting to such laws as might check so very pernicious a commerce.''

It was not until the following year that the Philadelphia petition to the Pennsylvania Assembly was gotten up, and it accords the credit to the Southern colony by asking similar action with that of ''the province of Virginia,

whose House of Burgesses have lately peti-
tioned the king.''

On the 5th of October, 1778, Virginia passed
an act forbidding the further importation of
slaves, *by land or water*, under a penalty of
£1000 from the seller and £500 from the buyer,
and freedom to the slave: thus giving to the
world the first example of an attempt by legislative enactment to destroy the slave trade.

When the vote was taken in the Federal Congress on the resolution to postpone the prohibition of the trade to the year 1808, Virginia
used all her influence to defeat the postpone-
ment, and it was carried by New Hamphire,
Massachusetts, and Connecticut voting with
Maryland, the Carolinas and Georgia. John
Adams, writing of a speech of James Otis in
1761, says: ''Nor were the poor negroes forgotten. Not a Quaker in Philadelphia, nor
Mr. Jefferson of Virginia, ever asserted the
rights of negroes in stronger terms. Young
as I was and ignorant as I was, I shuddered
at the doctrine he taught.''

The final prohibition of the slave trade by
act of Congress was brought about through the
influence of President Jefferson and by the active efforts of Virginians. And greatly to the

labors of the representatives from Virginia was due the final extinction of the vile traffic through the act of Congress declaring it to be piracy, five years before Great Britain took similar action with regard to her subjects.

Such is the actual record of the much-vilified South relating to the African slave trade, taken from officials records.

Now as to slavery itself. We have seen how it was brought upon the South without its fault, and continued to be forced upon her against her protests. Let us for a moment investigate the facts connected with its continuance.

The gradual system of emancipation adopted at the North had undoubtedly led to many of the slaves being shipped off to the South and sold. When, therefore, after this "abolition," the movement, from being confined to the comparatively small band of liberators who were actuated by pure principle, extended to those who had been their persecutors, it aroused a suspicion at the South which blinded it to a just judgment of the case.

If the South maintained slavery unjustifiably, during its continuance, instead of its unnecessary horrors being, as is popularly believed,

37

augmented by the natural brutality of the
Southerner, the real facts are that the system
was at the South perhaps fraught with less
atrocity than it was whilst it continued at the
North.

In the earliest period of the institution it
was justified on the ground of the slaves being
heathen, and a doubt was raised whether baptism would not operate to emancipate. At the
South it was adjudicated that it did not so operate; but long prior to this act negroes were admitted to the Church. In the leading colony
at the North baptism was at the time expressly
prohibited. The necessary concomitants of
slavery were wretched enough, and the continuance of the system proved the curse of the
fair land where it flourished, but to the African
himself it was a blessing; it gave his race the
only civilization it has had since the dawn of
history.

The statutory laws relating to slavery at the
South are held up as proof of the brutality with
which they were treated even under the law.
But these laws were not more cruel than were
the laws of England at the period when they
were enacted; they were rarely put into practical execution; and at least Southerners never

tolerated wholesale burning at the stake as a legal punishment, as was done in New York as late as 1741, when fourteen negroes were burnt at the stake on the flimsy testimony of a half-crazy servant girl; and as was done in Massachusetts as late as 1755, when a negro was burnt for murder.

In the cotton and sugar States, where the negroes were congregated in large numbers, and where a certain degree of absenteeism prevailed, there was naturally and necessarily more hardship.

African slavery was tolerated in Virginia and the Carolinas, but it received its first express legislative sanction from the Commonwealth of Massachusetts.

This Commonwealth, which has done so much to advance civilization, must bear the distinction of being the first American colony to proclaim slavery; to endorse the slave trade by legal sanction, and to build and equip the first slave-ship which sailed from an American port. Even the *Mayflower,* whose timbers one might have supposed would be regarded as sanctified by the holy fathers whose feet first touched Plymouth Rock, was, according to tradition, turned to a more secular use, and is reported by general tradition to have been subsequently employed as an African slaver. Whether this be true or not, the first American slaver was the Salem ship *The Desire*, which was built and equipped at Marblehead in 1636, and was the prototype of a long line of slavers, in which, through many decades, continuing long after slavery was abolished in New England, and after the Southern States were piling protest on protest and act on act to inhibit the slave trade, New England shippers, in violation of law, plied their hellish traffic between the African coast and the slave-holding countries.

Whatever may have been the horrors of African slavery in the South, it was in its worst form and under its most inhuman surroundings a mild and beneficent system, benevolent in its features and philanthropic in its characteristics, when compared with the slave trade itself. The horrors of "the middle passage," when human beings, often to the number of eight or nine hundred, were "piled almost in bulk on water-casks," or were packed between the hatches in a space where there was "not room for a man to sit unless inclining his head forward, their food half a pint of rice per day, with one pint of water," with "a blazing sun above, the boiling sea beneath, a withering air around," had never been equaled before, and in the providence of God will never be again.

It is not necessary to defend slavery, to defend the race which found it thrust upon it, contrary to what it deemed its rights, and which, after long and futile effort to rid itself of it, in accordance with what it held to be consistent at once with its rights and its security, refused to permit any outside interference. This was not primarily because it was wedded to slavery, but because it tolerated no invasion of its rights under any form or upon any pretext.

Vermont was the first State to lead off with emancipation in 1777. By the census of 1790 but seventeen slaves remained in the State. New Hampshire and Massachusetts failed to fix a statutory period; but the census of 1790 gives the former State 158 slaves, "and one of these was still reported in 1840."

Rhode Island and Connecticut about the same time adopted a gradual plan of emancipation. The latter State held 2,759 slaves in 1790—too many to admit of immediate emancipation.

Pennsylvania had by the same census 3,737 slaves, and, recognizing the peril of injecting such a number of freedmen into the body politic, provided in 1780, by an act said to have been drafted by Benjamin Franklin, that all slaves born after that time should be free when they attained the age of twenty-eight years. The census of 1840 showed sixty-four still held in slavery.

In New York, by an act passed in 1799, the future issue of slaves were set free—males at the age of twenty-eight and females at the age of twenty-five years. In 1790 there were 21,324 slaves in the State. In 1800, before the act of emancipation could take effect, this number had fallen off 981.

New Jersey in 1790 held 11,433 slaves. In 1804 her act of gradual emancipation was adopted. She had 674 slaves in 1840 and 236 in 1850.

This movement was largely owing in its inception to the efforts of the Quakers, who have devoted to peace those energies which others have given to war, and who have ever been moved by the spirit to take the initiative in all action which tends to the amelioration of the condition of the human race.

While this spirit of emancipation was passing over the North, the South, to whose action in asserting general freedom and universal civil equality was due the impulse, was stirring in the same direction. With her, however, the problem was far more difficult of solution, and although she addressed herself to it with energy and sincerity, she proved finally unequal to the task, and it was reserved, in the providence of an all-wise God, for the bitter scalpel of war to remove that which had served its purpose and was slowly sapping the life-blood of the South.

In the New England and Northern States, there were, by the census of 1790, less than 42,000 slaves: in Virginia alone, by the same census, there were 293,427 slaves—about seven times the number contained in all the others put together.

How were they to be freed with advantage to the slaves and security to the State?

John Randolph of Roanoke described the situation aptly when he said we were holding a wolf by the ears, and it was equally dangerous to let go and to hold on.

The problem was stupendous. But it was not despaired of. Many masters manumitted their slaves, the example being set by numbers of the same benevolent sect to which reference has been made. By the census of 1781 there were in Virginia 12,866 free negroes. Schemes of general emancipation of the slaves in Virginia had been proposed to the legislature by Jefferson in 1776; by William Craighead, and by Dr. William Thornton in 1785, whilst other schemes were proposed by St. George Tucker in 1796, by Thomas Jefferson Randolph in 1832, and by others from time to time. The vast body of slaves in the country, however, rendered it a matter so perilous as to prevent the schemes from ever being effectuated.

The most feasible plan appeared to be one that should lead to the colonization of the race in Africa; and the American Colonization Society was organized in Washington on the 1st of January, 1817, with Bushrod Washington president, and William H. Crawford, Henry Clay, John Taylor, and General John Mason, John Eager Howard, Samuel F. Smith, and John C. Herbert of Maryland, and Andrew Jackson of Tennessee among its vice-presidents.

Auxiliary societies were organized all over Virginia, John Marshall being the president of that established in Richmond, and ex-Governors Pleasants and Tyler being vice-presidents. James Madison, James Monroe, and John Tyler all threw the weight of their great influence to carry out the purposes of the society and make it successful. Strange to say, every act on the part of the South leading towards liberation was viewed with suspicion by the Abolitionists of the North, and every step in that direction was opposed by them. Later a new and independent State organization was formed, called the Colonization Society of Virginia. Its president was John Marshall; its vice-presidents, James Madison, James Monroe, James Pleasants, John Tyler, Hugh Nelson, and others; and its roll of membership embraced the most influential men in the State.

Everything was looking towards the gradual but final extinction of African slavery. It was prevented by the attitude of the Northern Abolitionists. Their furious onslaughts, accompanied by the illegal circulation of literature calculated to excite the negroes to revolt, and by the incursions of emissaries whose avowed object was the liberation of the slaves, but the effect of whose action was the instigation of the race to rise and fling off the yoke by rebellion and murder, chilled this feeling, the balance of political power came into question, and the temper of the South changed.

From this movement dates the unremittingly hostile attitude of the two sections towards each other. Before there had been antagonism; now there was open hostility. Before there had been conflicting rights, but they had been compromised and adjusted; from this time there was no compromise. The Northerner was a "miserable Yankee" and the Southerner was a "brutal slave-holder."

The two sections grew to be as absolutely separated as though a sea rolled between them. The antagonism increased steadily and became intensified. It extended far beyond the original cause, and finally became a factor in every problem, social and political, which existed in the whole land, affecting its results and often controlling its solution; forcing the two sections wider and wider apart, and eventually dividing them by an impassable gulf. Slavery, the prime cause, sank into insignificance in the multitudinous and potent differences which reared themselves between the two sections. It was employed simply as the battle-cry of the two opponents who stood arrayed against each other on a much broader question. The real fight was whether the conservative South should, with its doctrine of States' rights, of original State sovereignty, rule the country according to a literal reading of the Constitution, or whether the North should govern according to a more liberal construction, adapted, as it claimed, by necessity to the new and more advanced conditions of the nation. Finally it culminated. After convulsions which would have long before destroyed a less stable nation, the explosion came.

The South, outraged at continual violation of the Constitution, declared that it would no longer act in unison with the North, and, after grave deliberation and hesitation, rendered proper by the magnitude of the step contemplated, the far Southern States exercised their sovereign right and dissolved their connection with the Union. Then came the President's call for troops, and finding themselves forced to secede or to make war upon their sister States, the border States withdrew.

The North made war upon the South, and, backed by the resources and the sentiment of the world, after four years compelled her to recede from her action.

Such in outline is the history of the South as it relates to slavery.

What has taken place since belongs partly to the New South and partly to the Old South.

The Old South made this people. One hundred years ago this nation, like Athene, sprang full panoplied from her brain.

It was the South that planned first the cooperation of the colonies, then their consolidation, and finally their establishment as free and independent States.

It was a Southerner, Henry, who first struck the note of independence. It was a Southerner, Nelson, who first moved, and the Convention of Virginia, a Southern colony, which first adopted the resolution "that the delegates appointed to represent this colony in General Congress be instructed to propose to that respectable body to declare the United Colonies free and independent States, absolved from all allegiance to or dependence on the crown or Parliament of Great Britain."

It was a Southern colony which first emblazoned on her standard the emblem of her principle, *Virginia for Constitutional Liberty*.

It was a Southerner who wrote the *Declaration of Independence*.

These acts created revolution, and a Southerner led the armies of the revolutionists to victory; and when victory had been won it was to Southern intellect and Southern patriotism which created the Federal Constitution, that was due the final consolidation of the separated and disjointed elements extended along the Atlantic coast into one grand union of republics known as the United States.

From this time the South was as prominent in the affairs of the nation as she had been when she stood, a rock of defence, between the encroachments of the crown and the liberties of the colonies.

Of the Presidents who had governed the United States up to the time of the Civil War, the Old South had contributed Washington, Jefferson, Madison, Monroe, Jackson, Harrison, Tyler, Polk, and Taylor, and the cabinets had been filled with the representatives of the same civilization. In the only two wars which had ruffled the peaceful surface of the nation's course during this period the leading generals had been Southerners, and of the Chief Justices, John Marshall and Roger B. Taney had presided successively over the supreme bench of the United States from 1801, bringing to bear upon the decisions of that tribunal the force of their great minds, and the philosophic thought which is characteristic of the civilization of which they were such distinguished exponents.

Next to George Washington, John Marshall probably did more than any other one man to establish the principles on which this government is founded; for by his decisions he settled the mutual rights of the States on a firm and equitable basis, and determined forever those questions which might have strained the bonds of the young government.

To the South is due the fact that Louisiana is not now a French republic, and that the Mississippi rolls its whole length through the free land of the United States; to the South that the vast empire of Texas is not a hostile government; to the South is due the establishment of this Union in its integrity, and of the doctrines upon which it is maintained.

Thus in the council chamber and the camp, in the forum or on the field of battle, opposing invading armies or fighting for those principles which are ingrained in the very web and woof of our national life, the representatives of that contemned civilization always took the lead. In the great Civil War the two greatest men who stood for the Union, and to whom its preservation was due, were in large part the product of this civilization. Both Grant and Lincoln—the great general and the still greater President—sprang from Southern loins.

Can the New South make a better showing than this, or trace its lineage to a stronger source?

But as grand as is this exhibition of her genius, this is not her best history. The record of battles and of splendid deeds may serve to arrest admiration and to mark the course of events, as the constellations in the arch above us appear to the beholder nobler than the infinite multitude of the stars that fill the boundless reaches between; but the true record of the life of that civilization is deeper and worthier than this.

As the azure fields that stretch away through space are filled with stars which refuse their individual rays to the naked eye, yet are ever sending light through all the boundless realms of space, so under this brilliant exhibition of the South's public career lies the record of a life, of a civilization so pure, so noble, that the world to-day holds nothing equal to it.

After less than a generation it has become among friends and enemies the recognized field of romance.

Its chief attribute was conservatism. Others were courage, fidelity, purity, hospitality, magnanimity, honesty, and truth.

Whilst it proudly boasted itself democratic,

it was distinctly and avowedly anti-radical—
holding fast to those things which were proved,
and standing with its conservatism a steadfast
bulwark against all novelties and aggressions.

No dangerous isms flourished in that placid
atmosphere; against that civilization innova-
tions beat vainly as the waves lash themselves
to spray against the steadfast shore.

Slavery itself, which proved the spring of
woes unnumbered, and which clogged the
wheels of progress and withdrew the South
from sympathy with the outer world, christianized a race and was the automatic balance-wheel
between labor and capital which prevented, on
the one hand, the excessive accumulation of
wealth, with its attendant perils, and on the
other hand prevented the antithesis of the immense pauper class which work for less than
the wage of the slave without any of his inci-
dental compensations.

In the sea-island cotton and rice districts, and
the sugar sections, it is true that there was a
class which accumulated wealth and lived in a
splendor unknown to the people of Virginia and
of the interior portions of the cotton and sugar
States; but the proportion of these to the entire
population of the South who in the aggregate

made up the Southern civilization is so small that it need scarcely be taken into account.

That the Southerner was courageous the whole world admits. His friends claim it; his foes know it. Probably never has such an army existed as that which followed Lee and Jackson from the time when, march-stained and battle-scarred, it flung itself across the swamps of the Chickahominy and stood a wall of fire between McClellan and the hard-pressed capital of the Confederate South.

It was not discipline, it was not *esprit de corps*, it was not traditional renown, it was not mere generalship which carried that army through. It was personal, individual courage and devotion to principle which welded it together and made it invincible, until it was almost extirpated.

The mills of battle and of grim starvation ground it into dust; yet even then there remained a valor which might well have inspired that famous legend which was one of the traditions of the conflict between the Church and its assailants in earlier ages, that after the destruction of their bodies their fierce and indomitable spirits continued the desperate struggle in the realms of air.

The tendency to hospitality was not local nor narrow; it was the characteristic of the entire people, and its concomitant was a generosity so general and so common in its application that it created the quality of magnanimity as a race characteristic.

It was these qualities to which the South was indebted for her controlling influence in the government of the country, throughout that long period which terminated only when the North abrogated the solemn compact which bound the two sections together.

No section of this country more absolutely, loyally, and heartily accepts the fact that slavery and secession can never again become practical questions in this land, than does that which a generation ago flung all its weight into the opposite scale. But to pretend that we did not have the legal, constitutional right to secede from the Union is to stultify ourselves in falsification of history.

If any portion of this nation doubt the South's devotion to the Union, let it attempt to impair the Union. If the South is ever to be once more the leader of this nation, she must cherish the traditional glory of her former station, and prove to the world that her revolution was not a rebellion, but was fought for a principle upon which she was established as her foundation-stone—the sacred right of self-government.

Government was the passion of the Southerner. Trained from his earliest youth by the care and mastery of slaves, and the charge of affairs which demanded the qualities of mastership, the control of men became habitual with him, and domination became an instinct. Consequently, the only fields which he regarded as desirable were those which afforded him the opportunity for its exercise.

Thus every young Southerner of good social connection who was too poor to live without work, or too ambitious to be contented with his plantation, devoted himself to the learned professions—the law being the most desirable as offering the best opportunity for forensic display, and being the surest stepping-stone to political preferment.

Being emotional and impulsive, the Southerner was as susceptible to the influences of rhetoric as was the Athenian, and public speaking was cultivated as always a necessary qualification for public position.

The South on this account became celebrated

for its eloquence, which, if somewhat fervid when judged by the severe standard of later criticism, was, when measured by its immediate effects, extraordinarily successful. It contributed to preserve through the decades preceding the war the supremacy of the slave-holding South, even against the rapidly growing aggressiveness of the North, with the sentiment of the modern world at its back.

It is not necessary to make reference to those orators who in the public halls of the nation, and in their native States, whenever questions of moment were agitated, evoked thunders of applause alike from rapturous friends and dazzled enemies. Their fame is now a part of the history of the country.

But in every circuit throughout the length and breadth of the South are handed down, even now, traditions of speakers who, by the impassioned eloquence of their appeals, carried juries against both law and evidence, or on the hustings, in political combat, swept away immense majorities by the irresistible impetuosity of their oratory.

That the Old South was honest, no sensible man who reads the history of that time can doubt, and no honest man will deny. Its whole course throughout its existence, whatever other criticism it may be subjected to, was one of honesty and of honor. Even under the perils of public life, which try men's souls, the personal integrity which was a fruit of the civilization in which it flourished was never doubted.

In confirmation of this proposition, appeal can be made with confidence to the history of the public men of the South. They were generally poor men, frequently reckless men, not infrequently insolvent men; but their bitterest enemies never aspersed their honesty.

There was not one of them who could not say, with Laurens of South Carolina, "I am a poor man—God knows I am a poor man; but your king is not rich enough to buy me!"

In this they were the representatives of their people. The faintest suspicion of delinquency in this respect would have blasted the chances of any man at the South, however powerful or however able he might have been, and have consigned him to everlasting infamy. Whatever assaults may be made on that civilization, its final defence is this: The men were honorable and the women pure. So highly were these qualities esteemed, that the aspersion of either was deemed sufficient cause to take life.

If it has appeared to modern civilization that life has not been held sufficiently sacred at the South, this may be urged in her defence: that a comparative statement, based on the statistics, does not show that homicide is, or has ever been, more general at the South than at the North, when all classes are embraced in the statement; and if it has been tolerated among the upper classes under a form which has now happily passed away, it was in obedience to a sentiment which although grossly abused, had this much justification—that it placed honor above even life.

The principal element of weakness in the civilization of the Old South was that it was not productive in material wealth. The natural agricultural resources of the country were so great and so suited to the genius of the people that there were no manufactures to speak of.

The tendency of the civilization was the reduction of everything to principles, and not to disturb them by experiment. In this way there was an enormous waste. The physical resources of the country and the intellectual resources of its people were equally subject to this fault.

Whilst oratory flourished to a greater extent

than under any other civilization which has existed since the invention of the printing-press, there was no Southern literature. Rather, there were no publishers and no public. There were critics who might have shone on the *Edinburgh Review*, and writers who might have made an Augustan literature; but the atmosphere was against them.

A Virginian farmer sat down and wrote the great Bill of Rights, the finest State paper ever penned on this continent; a Virginian was called on to draft a paper in the absence of another who was to have drawn it, and he wrote the Declaration of Independence. Another, a naval officer, laid down the laws of the winds and tides, and charted the pathless deep into highways, so that men come and go as securely as on dry land. There was genius enough, but the spirit of the time was against it. In the main the authors wrote for their diversion, and the effort was not repeated. The environments were not conducive to literary production, and it was not called into being. The harpers were present at the feast, but no one called for the song.

It was to this that the South owed her final defeat. It was for lack of a literature that she was left behind in the great race for outside support, and that in the supreme moment of her existence she found herself arraigned at the bar of the world without an advocate and without a defence.

Only study the course of the contest against the South and you cannot fail to see how she was conquered by the pen rather than by the sword; and how unavailing against the resources of the world, which the North commanded through the sympathy it had enlisted, was the valiance of that heroic army, which, if courage could have availed, had withstood the universe.

That Southern army was worn away as a blade is worn by use and yet retains its temper while but a fragment exists.

When the supreme moment came, the South had the world against her; the North had brought to its aid the sympathy of Christendom, and its force was as the gravitation of the earth —imperceptible, yet irresistible.

From their standpoint they were right, as we were right from ours. Slavery was a great barrier which kept out the light, and the North wrote of us in the main only what it believed.

If it was ignorant, it is our fault that it was

not enlightened. We denied and fought, but we did not argue. Be this, however, our justification, that slavery did not admit of argument. Argument meant destruction.

The future historian of the Old South and of its civilization is yet to arise.

If in this audience to-night there be any young son of the South in whose veins there beats the blood of a soldier who perilled his life for that civilization which has been so inadequately outlined, and who, as he had heard from his mother's lips the story of his father's glorious sacrifice, has felt his pulses throb and his heart burn with noble aspiration, let him know that though he may never, like his father, be called upon to defend his principles with his life, yet he has before him a work not less noble, a career not less glorious: the true recording of that story, of that civilization whose history has never yet been written—the history of the Old South.

What nobler task can he set himself than this—to preserve from oblivion, or worse, from misrepresentation, a civilization which produced as its natural fruit Washington and Lee!

It is said that in all history there is no finer flight of human eloquence than that in which the Athenian orator aroused his countrymen by his appeal to the spirits of their sires who fell at Marathon. Shall not some one preserve the history of our fathers who fell in what they deemed a cause as sacred? Can any good come forth of a generation that believe that their fathers were traitors? I thank God that the sword of the South will nevermore be drawn except in defence of this Union; but I thank God equally that it is now without a stain. The time will come when the North as well as the South shall know that this Union is more secure because of the one heritage that our fathers have left us—the heritage of an untarnished sword.

If he shall feel the impulse stirring in his bosom to consecrate to this work the powers which have been nurtured at the nourishing breasts of this bountiful mother, there can be no fitter place for his sacrament than these hallowed walls—no better time than the present.

Within these sacred precincts three monuments meet his gaze. Each of them, by coincidence, is dedicated to the memory of one who had learnt by heart the lesson which that history teaches when rightly read,—the devotion of life to duty.

One of these was the leader of armies, the noblest character the South has produced, the great Lee; who, putting aside proffers of wealth and place and honor, gave himself to teaching the South the sublime beauty of devotion to duty—that lesson whose most admirable example was his own life. One was the surgeon, James M. Ambler, who refused to accept his life, and died amid the snows of the Lena Delta, pistol in hand, guarding the bodies of his dead comrades. Who does not remember the story of the young surgeon, kneeling amid the perpetual snows, pointing his dying comrades to Christ the crucified! The third, William E. Lynch, was a student, who while yet a lad put into action the same divine lesson, and to save a fellow-student plunged dauntless into the icy river and died, while yet a boy, a hero's death. All three speak to us this evening with sublime eloquence the heroic story of the Old South!

Here within these sacred walls, where the foremost soldier, the knightliest gentleman, the noblest man of his race, taught his sublime lesson, and his pupils learned to put it into such divine practice, the heart cannot but feel that the true story of their life must be told, the song must be sung, through the ages.

Not far off repose the ashes of another great soldier, Stonewall Jackson, the representative of the element that settled this valley, as Lee was representative of that which settled the tide-water. He flashed across the sky, a sudden meteor, and expired with a fame for brilliancy second only to Napoleon.

Near by him, and side by side with his own only son, Stonewall Jackson's aide-de-camp, Colonel Alexander S. Pendleton, slain in battle at the age of twenty-three, lies one to whom I owe a personal debt which I desire to acknowledge publicly to-night: General William Nelson Pendleton, a soldier who doffed the cassock for the uniform, and who lived a warrior-priest, leading his men in peace as he had done in war, and like his old commander, the highest type of the Christian soldier.

Standing here beside the sacred ashes of the noblest exponent of that civilization, which I have attempted to outline, delivering my message from this University, his grandest monument, I hail the future historian of the Old South.

AUTHORSHIP IN THE SOUTH
BEFORE THE WAR

AUTHORSHIP IN THE SOUTH BEFORE THE WAR

DISCUSSION of Southern literature during the period which preceded the late war naturally resolves itself into a consideration of the causes which retarded its growth, since the absence of a literature at the South during a period so prolific in intellectual energy of a different kind, is one of the notable conditions of a civilization which was as remarkable in many respects as any that has existed in modern times.

The object of this paper is to set forth the probable causes which conduced to this absence of literature, to place the responsibility where it properly belongs, and at the same time to direct attention to those courageous spirits who, imbued with love of Literature for herself alone, against the inexorable destiny of the time, unrecognized and unencouraged, aspired and struggled to give the South a literature of her own.

The limitations of this paper, which it is proposed to devote to the development of work of a purely literary character, preclude the possibility of embracing in it any discussion or even mention of professional and economical works, which constitute so large a proportion of the writings of the South,—such, for example, as the writings of Washington, Jefferson, Madison, John Taylor, Calhoun, Benton, Rivers, Legaré, Scott, and others; the legal works of the Tuckers, Lomax, Holcomb, Davis, Robinson, Benjamin, Minor, Daniel, and others; the scientific works of Audubon, Wilson, the Le Contes, Courtenay, Talcott, and others; the works of the great Maury; the historical works of writers in nearly every Southern State; the philosophical works of the Alexanders, Bledsoe, Breckinridge, Thornwell, and many others. Owing to the environment, much the larger portion of the writing done by the South was philosophical or polemical, only a small portion being purely literary.

It has been generally charged, and almost universally believed, that the want of a literature at the South was the result of intellectual poverty. The charge, however, is without foundation, as will be apparent to any fair-minded student who considers the position held by the South not only during the period of the formation of the government, but also throughout the long struggle between the South and the North over the momentous questions generated by the institution of slavery. In the former crisis the South asserted herself with a power and wisdom unsurpassed in the history of intellectual resource; throughout the latter period she maintained the contest with consummate ability and with transcendent vigor of intellect.

The causes of the absence of a Southern literature are to be looked for elsewhere than in intellectual indigence. The intellectual conditions were such as might well have created a noble literature, but the physical conditions were adverse to its production and were too potent to be overcome.

The principal causes were the following:—

1. The people of the South were an agricultural people, widely diffused, and lacking the stimulus of immediate mental contact.

2. The absence of cities, which in the history of literary life have proved literary foci essential for its production, and the want of publishing-houses at the South.

3. The exactions of the institution of slavery,

and the absorption of the intellectual forces of the people of the South in the solution of the vital problems it engendered.

4. The general ambition of the Southern people for political distinction, and the application of their literary powers to polemical controversy.

5. The absence of a reading public at the South for American authors, due in part to the conservatism of the Southern people.

Instead of being settled in towns and communities, as was the case at the North, the bent of the people from the first was to hold land in severalty in large bodies, and to continue the manorial system after the custom of their fathers and their kinsmen in the old country, with whom they even after the Revolution still kept up a sort of traditional association. The possession of slaves, often in large numbers, and the imperative responsibilities of their regulation and no less of their protection which such possession entailed, fostered this inherent tendency and eventually made the Southern people[1] agricultural to the almost total exclusion of manufactures.

[1] It is well to remember that this term ''the Southern people,'' although *ex vi termini* general in its meaning, is applicable in

AUTHORSHIP IN THE SOUTH

No merely agricultural people has ever produced a literature. It would appear that for the production of literature some centre is requisite, where men with literary instincts may commingle, and where their thought may be focussed.

The life of the South was in the fields, and its population was so diffused that there was always lacking the mental stimulus necessary

this paper and in all discussion of this subject only to the landowning or better class of whites, as contra-distinguished not only from the negroes, but also from the lower class of whites, who neither possessed the advantages nor incurred the responsibilities of the upper class.

This distinction is ordinarily overlooked in the discussion of this matter. The importance of the limitation will be apparent, however, when it is considered that by the census of 1850 (which is assumed as a fair standard because then the growth of literature at the North was about at its zenith) the entire slave-holding and slave-hiring population of the South was only 347,525.

This embraces all white artisans and working people, whether in the towns or in the rural districts, who hired one negro servant.

This was the population of the South from which alone could spring a literature. Nothing was to be expected from the lower class of poor whites, and, of course, nothing from the negroes, for they had no advantages of education, a large percentage of the former, and nearly all of the latter, being unable to read and write.

This ignorance on the part of the lower classes was a necessary concomitant of slavery, for which institution, notwithstanding the long-established popular belief of the outside world, the South was not responsible.

to the production of a literature. There were few towns, and yet fewer cities. But these few —Baltimore, New Orleans, Charleston, Richmond, and Louisville—all attested the truth of this observation. From them radiated the occasional beams of light which illumined the general darkness of the period, and there from time to time appeared the infallible signs of literary germination, in the form of magazines, which, struggling against adverse influences, unhappily perished in the process of birth or faded untimely in early youth. For example, *Niles's Register*, which was the first magazine of any permanence, was published in Baltimore from 1811 to 1849. The Pinkneys,—Edward Coate, William, and Ninian,—John P. Kennedy, Francis Scott Key, and others received its vivifying influence. Elliot's and Legaré's *Southern Review* was conducted in Charleston from 1828 to 1832, and was followed in 1835 by *The Southern Literary Journal*, which existed only two years, and in its turn after an interval was succeeded in 1842 by *The Southern Quarterly Review*, which expired in 1856. Besides which, there was Simms's *Southern and Western Magazine and Review*. After these the earnest Hayne established *Russell's Magazine*. These literary ventures, with a dozen or so of less note, such as *The Southern Literary Gazette*, *The Cosmopolitan*, *The Magnolia*, etc., contributed to the evolution and development of William Gilmore Simms, Hugh S. Legaré, Paul H. Hayne, the Timrods, Porcher, De Bow, and others, and became the organs of their thought. They created a literary atmosphere of a higher quality than existed generally, and supported the claim of Charleston to be the chief literary focus of the South. *De Bow's Review*, though scarcely to be classed as a mere literary exponent, yet with other transitory periodicals subserved the literary spirit of New Orleans from 1846 to the outbreak of the war.

The nascent literary feeling of the West found expression for a brief period in the *Western Review* in Lexington, Kentucky, but was not strong enough to maintain it above a year. But George D. Prentice opened the *Courier Journal* to literary aspiration, and made Louisville the literary centre of that section. The genius of Prentice himself found an outlet in his columns, and the instinct of many others, such as O'Hara, the poetess Amelia B. Welby, Mrs. Betts, Mrs. Warfield, and Mrs.

Jeffrey, was inspired by Prentice's sympathy and fostered by his encouragement.

In Richmond, Virginia, appeared perhaps the most noted literary magazine which the South produced,—*The Southern Literary Messenger*. It was undertaken as a mere business venture in 1835, and through the inspiring genius of Poe, who began immediately to write for it and shortly became its editor, it promised for a time to bring a literature into being. Although it was supported by the best literary writers not only of Virginia but of the South and survived until 1864, like its fellows it contended against forces too potent to be successfully resisted, and never attained a very high mark of literary merit. However, it had much to do with sustaining the unstable Poe, and with developing nearly all of those writers of the South whose names have survived.

The editors of these periodicals appear to have possessed a sufficiently correct appreciation of what was requisite, and to have striven bravely enough to attain it; but failure was their invariable lot. They besought their contributors to abandon the servile copying of English models and address themselves to the portrayal of the life around them with which they were familiar; they enlisted whatever literary ability there was to be secured; but they received no encouragement and met with no success.

The habits of life and the exigencies of life at the South were against them.

The constituency which should have sustained them was not only too widely diffused, but was too intent on the solution of the vital problems which faced it at its own doors, to give that fostering encouragement which literary aspiration in its first beginning absolutely demands. The South was so unremittingly exercised in considering and solving the questions which slavery was ever raising that it had neither time nor opportunity, if it had the inclination, to apply itself to other matters. The intellectual powers of the South were absorbingly devoted to this subject, and in consequence of the exigencies of life at the South generally took the direction of spoken and not of written speech. Where writing was indulged in, it was almost invariably of the philosophical, polemical character.

"Literature," says Carlyle, "is the thought of thinking souls." Accepting this definition, the South was rich in literature. There was sufficient poetry and wisdom delivered on the porticos and in the halls of the Southern people to have enriched the age, had it but been transmitted in permanent form; but wanting both the means and the inclination to put it in an abiding form, they were wasted in discourse or were spent in mere debate.

Owing to the position which the South occupied because of the institution of slavery and the difficulties engendered by that institution, the whole fabric of life at the South was infused with politics, and oratory was universally cultivated. Thus the profession of the law, which afforded the opportunity at once for the practice and for the application of oratory, and which was the chief highway to political preferment, became the general avenue by which all aspiring genius sought to achieve power and fame, and writing was in consequence neglected, as too indirect a mode to accomplish the desired end.

There was much writing done, but it was of the kind which is not deemed incompatible with proper loyalty to the law, taking the invariable form of political disquisition or of polemical discussion. In these, indeed, the Southerner indefatigably indulged, and attained a rare degree of perfection. Thus, the philosophical works of such men as Madison, John Taylor of Caroline, Calhoun, etc., and the public prints of the day generally, exhibit powers which abundantly refute the charge that the absence of a literature was due to mental poverty. In the city of Richmond alone were four writers for the daily press whose brilliant work is a guarantee of the success they would have achieved in any department of literature they might have chosen. These were Thomas Ritchie, John Hampden Pleasants, Edward T. Johnston, and John M. Daniel. In their time the editorial columns of the *Enquirer, Whig,* and *Examiner* possessed a potency which is at this time well-nigh inconceivable. They may be said to have almost controlled the destinies of the great political parties of the country. The *Whig* and the *Enquirer* were the bitterest antagonists, their hostility resulting finally in a fatal duel between Pleasants, the editor of the *Whig,* and a son of his rival, "Mr. Ritchie," of the *Enquirer.* But this antagonism may be as well shown by a less tragic illustration: the *Enquirer* was accustomed to publish original poetry in a column at the head of which stood the legend, "Much yet remains unsung"; the

Whig kept standing a notice that "poetry" would be published at a dollar a line.

It would indeed appear that, with the potency of intellectual demonstration so constantly and so forcibly illustrated throughout the land, the Southerner would have been irresistibly impelled to seek a wider field, a more extensive audience, and would inevitably have sought to put into permanent form the product of his mind.

What might not the eloquence and genius of Clay have effected had they been turned in the direction of literature, or what the mental acumen, the philosophic force, the learning of Calhoun, of whom Dr. Dwight said when he left college that the young man knew enough to be President of the United States! How much did literature lose when Marshall, Wirt, the Lees, Martin, Pinkney, Berrien, Hayne, Preston, Cobb, Clingman, Ruffin, Legaré, Soulé, Davis, Roane, Johnston, Crittenden, devoted all their brilliant powers to politics and the law! John Randolph boasted that he should "go down to the grave guiltless of rhyme," yet his letters contain the concentrated essence of intellectual energy; his epigrams stung like a branding-iron, and are the current coin of tra-

dition throughout his native State two generations after his death.

Literature stood no chance because the ambition of young men of the South was universally turned in the direction of political distinction, and because the monopoly of advancement held by the profession of the law was too
well established and too clearly recognized to
admit of its claim being contested; and once
in the service of the law there be few with
either the inclination or the courage to assert
any independence. Even now the Southerner
will not believe that a man can be a lawyer
and an author. Yet it was not unnatural that
the major portion of such literary work as was
done at the South was done by lawyers.

Their profession called forth the exercise of
the highest intellectual powers, and necessarily
they occasionally strayed into the adjoining domain of letters. The pity of it is that their
literary work was in the main but the desul-
tory "jottings down" in their hours of recrea-
tion of fragmentary sketches, which were usually based on the humorous phases of life with
which their profession made them familiar, and
almost the best is stamped with the mark of an
apparent dilettanteism.

Chief Justice Marshall took time to write a life of Washington, but there was little biography attempted. William Wirt early in the century entertained himself amid the exactions of practice by contributing to the Richmond *Argus* "The Letters of a British Spy," and subsequently wrote his "Old Bachelor" and his "Life of Patrick Henry," on the last of which his present fame rests more than on his reputation as a great lawyer, even though he was one of the most distinguished advocates the nation has produced, was counsel in the most celebrated case which the legal annals of the country contain, and was among the ablest Attorney-Generals of the United States. Indeed, almost the only recollection of the great Burr trial which survives to the general public is the extract from Wirt's speech, preserved as a literary fragment, describing the Isle of Blennerhassett. Happily for his fame, Wirt held that, though a lawyer should strive to be a great lawyer, yet he should not be "a mere lawyer."

Among other writers of the South who were lawyers were the Tuckers of Virginia,—St. George (Sr.), who was a poet and an essayist as well as a jurist, George, the essayist, Henry St. George, Nathaniel Beverley, author of "The

Partisan Leader,'' and St. George (Jr.), author of ''Hansford, a Tale of Bacon's Rebellion.'' There was also John Pendleton Kennedy, of Maryland. These might have retrieved the reputation of the South in respect to literature if the Tuckers had not devoted all their best energies to the law, and if Kennedy had not been, as Poe said of him, ''over head and ears in business'' relating to the bar, his seat in Congress, and his seat in the Cabinet.

William Gilmore Simms began life as a lawyer, but his love for literature proved irrepressible, and in an evil hour for his material welfare he abandoned the profession and devoted himself to literature.

Others who were lawyers were Richard Henry Wilde, the poet, Joseph G. Baldwin, author of ''Flush Times of Alabama and Mississippi,'' Augustus B. Longstreet, author of ''Georgia Scenes,'' Philip Pendleton Cooke, the poet, John Esten Cooke, the novelist, the Pinkneys, Edward Coate and Frederick, Francis Scott Key, Thomas Hart Benton, Hugh Swinton Legaré, Alexander B. Meek, Francis Gilmer, the essayist, Charles Etienne Arthur Gayarré, the historian, dramatist, and novelist, Henry Timrod, Paul H. Hayne, John R

Thompson, James Barron Hope, and many others.

It is a full list, nearly complete, and comprises poets, novelists, essayists, and historians. Poe and Lanier were almost the only notable exceptions. With Poe, as he declared, poetry was "not a purpose, but a passion"; and in whatever else his besetting weakness made him fickle, he at least never wavered in his loyalty to his first and best love.

It was not remarkable that the law was preferred to literature, for in sober truth it required sterner stuff than most men were compounded of, and a more absorbing passion than most men were animated by, to follow literature as a pursuit. To do so was to take the vow of poverty. When Poe, even after having made a name, was receiving only four dollars and a half per printed magazine page for his marvellous work; when as editor of the magazine he thought himself generously rewarded by a salary of $520 per annum; when "The Gold-Bug," written at almost the height of his fame, brought only $52 and "The Raven" only $10, it must have been apparent to every sensible man that, whatever the rewards of literature might be, a reasonable support was not among them. Reducing the question to the unromantic level of fair compensation, there were few who were willing to give for a contingent interest in a niche of Fame's temple, which, in the language of the law, was, at best, *potentia remotissima*, the bread and butter and bonnets and equipages which were assured at the bar.

William Gilmore Simms, who was one of the very first who had the temerity to brave the hardships of a literary life, complained that he had never held the position which rightfully belonged to him, because he made his living as a writer.

The responsibility for the want of a literature was not with the writers, but with the environment. There was lacking not only the mental stimulus of contact between mind and mind, but also that yet more essential inspiration, sympathy with literary effort, which is as necessary to literary vitality as the atmosphere is to physical existence. One of Philip Pendleton Cooke's neighbors said to him after he became known as the author of "Florence Vane," "I would n't waste time on a damned thing like poetry: you might make yourself, with all your sense and judgment, a useful man in settling neighborhood disputes and difficulties."

It is matter for little wonder that the poet declared that one had as much chance with such people as a dolphin would have if in one of his darts he pitched in among the machinery of a mill.

As a consequence of the South's position during this period, there was another barrier to literature. The standard of literary work was not a purely literary standard, but one based on public opinion, which in its turn was founded on the general consensus that the existing institution was not to be impugned, directly or indirectly, on any ground or by any means whatsoever.

This was an atmosphere in which literature could not flourish. In consequence, where literature was indulged in it was in a half-apologetic way, as if it were not altogether compatible with the social dignity of the author. Thought which in its expression has any other standard than fidelity to truth, whatever secondary value it may have, cannot possess as much value as literature. "The Partisan Leader" was secretly printed in 1836, and was afterwards suppressed. It was again republished just before the beginning of the war, and was a second time suppressed or withdrawn. Augustus B. Longstreet, although he subsequently became a preacher, was at the bar when he wrote ''Georgia Scenes.'' He was so ashamed of having been beguiled into writing what is one of the raciest books of sketches yet produced, a book by which alone his name is now preserved, that he made a strenuous effort to secure and suppress the work after its publication. Even Richard Henry Wilde, who was a poet, and who should have possessed a poet's love for his art, did not conceive his best poem, ''My Life is Like the Summer Rose,'' worthy of acknowledgment. It was ''The Lament of the Captive'' in an epic poem which was never finished, and was published without his authority, and he was hardly persuaded to assert his claim to its authorship when, after it had been for a score of years merely ''attributed'' to him in this country, and in Great Britain had been known and admired as ''a poem by an American lawyer,'' it was unblushingly claimed and stolen by several more ambitious versifiers, who, if they failed to recognize the obligation of the eighth commandment, at least appreciated the value of literary talent higher than the real poet. The poem was as a hoax translated into Greek by

Barclay, of Savannah, and was attributed to a poet called Alcæus, and a controversy having arisen as to whether it was really written by an Irishman named O'Kelly, who had published it in a volume of his poems as his, or whether he had stolen it from the old Greek, Mr. Wilde, who was then a member of Congress from Georgia, was finally induced to admit that he had written the poem twenty years before. This he did in a letter characteristic of the time, declaring that he valued "these rhymes" very differently from others, and avowed their authorship only in compliance with the wishes of those he esteemed.

This attitude on the part of the South, taken in connection with the diffusion of its population, furnishes the only reasonable solution of the singular fact that the South produced so little literature notwithstanding its culture; for culture it possessed, and of the best kind,—the culture of the classics, the most fertilizing of all intellectual forces. If the lower classes were ignorant, the upper classes universally emphasized the distinction between them by giving their children the best education that could be obtained. Jefferson deplored the fact that over one-half of the students at Princeton were Virginians, and he founded the University of Virginia that Southerners might be able to secure the best education at home. Upon this sure foundation of a university training was laid the superstructure of constant association with the best classical authors.

These established the standard, and the Southerner held in contempt any writer who did not at once conform to their style and equal their merit.

Poe in his early manhood bitterly declared that "one might suppose that books, like their authors, improve by travel, their having crossed the sea is with us so great a distinction."

To any good in what was penned and published on this side the Atlantic the Southerner was, as a general thing, absolutely and incurably blind. If the work was written south of Mason and Dixon's line it was incontinently contemned as "trashy"; if it emanated from the North, it was vehemently denounced as "Yankee." In either case it was condemned.

With this in mind, it is not surprising that, with all the intellectual resources of the South, so few writers should have been found with the inclination or the temerity to attempt a work thus sure to terminate in failure, if not to incur contempt. If one should attempt it, where could he secure a publisher? There were few at the South, and to seek a publisher at the North was to hazard repulse there and insure criticism at home.

Thus, the true explanation of the absence of a Southern literature of a high order during this epoch was not the want of literary ability. There was genius enough to have founded a literature, but there were no publishers generally, and there was never any public.

Yet from the untoward conditions delineated issued a literary genius of the first rank.

Notwithstanding the coldness and indifference which he encountered in this State, Poe ever declared himself a Virginian; and, with all due respect to certain latter-day critics, who assert the contrary, it must be said that to those familiar with the qualities and with the points of difference between the Northern and Southern civilizations, Poe's poems are as distinctly Southern in their coloring, tone, and temper, as Wordsworth's are English. The wild landscape, the flower-laden atmosphere, the delirious richness, are their setting, and a more than tropical passion interfuses them as unmistakably as the air of English lawns and meadows

breathes through Tennyson's masterpieces. We
find in them everywhere

> Dim vales and shadowy floods,
> And cloudy-looking woods,
> Whose forms we can't discover
> For the trees that drip all over.

Poe, however, was limited by no boundary,
geographical or other. The spirit-peopled air,
the infernal chambers of fancied inquisitions,
the regions of the moon, the imagined horrors
of post mortem sentience, were equally his
realm. In all his vast and weird and wonderful
genius roamed unconfined and equally at home.
In all he created his own atmosphere, and projected his marvellous fancies with an originality
and a power whose universal application is the
undeniable and perfect proof of his supreme
genius.

That he failed of his immediate audience
was due, in part, to his own unfortunate disposition, but yet more to the time and to the blind-
ness which visited upon works of incomparable
literary merit the sins of physical frailty: the
creations of his genius, by reason of their very
originality, were contemned as the ravings of a
disordered and unbalanced mind, and, unrec-

ognized at home, Poe was forced to wander to an alien clime in search of bread.

With his personal habits this paper is not concerned. His life has been for more than a generation the object of attack and vituperation which have raged with inconceivable violence. From the time that Griswold perpetrated his "immortal infamy," vindictiveness has found in Poe's career its most convenient target. Yet the works of this unfortunate have caught the human heart, and are to-day the common property of the English-speaking races, whether dwelling in Virginia or Massachusetts, Great Britain or Australia, and have been translated into the language of every civilized nation of Europe. A recent review with the English publishers, the Routledges, showed that twenty-nine thousand copies of Poe's Tales had been sold by them in the year 1887, as against less than one-third of that number of many of the most popular and famous of our other American writers.

The obligation to Poe has never been duly recognized. It is said that the Latin poems of Milton first opened the eyes of the Italians to the fact that the island which Cæsar had conquered had become civilized. The first evidence of culture which was accepted abroad, after the long night of silence which covered the South after the departure of the great fathers of the Republic, was the work of Edgar A. Poe. It is not more to the credit of the North than of the South, that when the latter threw him off starving, the former failed to give him more than a crust.

"The Raven" created a sensation, and still thrills every poetic mind with wonder at its marvellous music and its mysterious power, but, though it secured for its author fame, it brought him only ten dollars' worth of bread. If literature has not advanced since that day, at least the welfare of literary men has done so. The writer of a short story or paper which is deemed worthy of a place in one of the modern monthly magazines of the better class, even though he may have no reputation, receives at least ten dollars per printed page; whilst, if he be at all well known, he may expect double or quadruple that sum. Poe received for some of his immortal works four dollars per printed page.

Poe's poetry discovered a fresh realm in the domain of fancy; but his prose works are, if possible, even more remarkable. His critical faculty installed a new era in criticism. Up to this time the literary press, too imbecile to possess, or too feeble to assert, independence, cringed fawning at the feet of every writer whose position was assured among what was recognized as the literary set, and accepted with laudation, or at least with flattering deference, all publications which bore the talismanic charm of an established name. Poe undoubtedly was at times too much influenced by personal feeling, but, with the courage of one who had vowed his life to truth, he stripped off the mask of dull respectability, and relentlessly exposed sham and vacuity under whatever name they appeared.

"If," as Mr. Lowell said, "he seems at times to mistake his vial of prussic acid for his inkstand," yet he lifted literary criticism from the abasement of snivelling imbecility into which it had sunk, and established it upon a basis founded on the principles of analysis, philosophy, and art.

If in discussing the works of female writers his susceptible nature and his chivalrous instinct unduly inclined him to bestow praise on what was mere trash, yet no less an authority than Mr. Lowell said of him that he was "the most discriminating, philosophical, and fearless critic upon imaginative works who has ever written in America.''

His own imaginative works created a new school, and have never been equalled in their peculiar vein, or surpassed in any vein whatever in the qualities of originality, force, and art.

Edgar A. Poe died at the age of thirty-nine, when the powers and faculties are just matured. What might he not have done had he lived out the full span of man's allotted life!

He was not prolific either in prose or in verse, his health or his habits frequently incapacitating him from work; but both his poems and his tales not only evince his genius, but exhibit the highest degree of literary art.

It has become the fashion to decry Poe and to disparage his work; but the detraction which has been expended upon him for a period extending over nearly two generations has only made his literary fame brighter. As Mr. Gosse has aptly said, he has been a veritable piper of Hamelin to all American writers since his time.

If we are compelled to admit that he is the one really great writer of purely literary work that the South produced under its old condi-

tions, it is no reflection on the South or its civilization, for the North during the same period,
with an educated population many times larger,
can claim only three or four, whilst England
herself, "with all appliances and means to
boot," can number hardly more than a score.

There were other writers besides Poe who
braved the chilling indifference of the time, and
who wrote and strove, devoting labor and life
to the endeavor to awake the South to a realiza-
tion of its literary abilities.

But few of them have survived to more than
mention in works of reference, and the most
that can be done is to mention those whose
work was distinctive in its character or scope,
or who by their diligence and ardor may be
deemed to have rewarded the cause of Southern literature.

Excepting Poe, who stands pre-eminent above
all others, the three leading literary men of the
South during the period which extended down
to the war were John Pendleton Kennedy, of
Maryland, William Gilmore Simms, of South
Carolina, and John Esten Cooke, of Virginia.

There were others who, in prose or in verse,
in a short sketch or a lyric, struck perhaps a
higher key than these did, but the effort was

rarely repeated, and these were the leading literary men of the South, not merely as authors, but as the friends and promoters of literature.

Of these Kennedy was first in time, whilst Simms was first in his devotion to literature and in the work he accomplished. Indeed, no one in the history of Southern literature ever applied himself more assiduously and loyally to its development than Simms. Both of these exercised a wider influence upon the literary spirit of the South than that which proceeded immediately from their works. Kennedy, who was born in 1795 in Baltimore, where he lived all of his long life, had not only made his mark as a lawyer and man of affairs, but as the author of "Swallow Barn" had already acquired a reputation as a literary man, when in the autumn of 1833 the two prizes offered by the proprietors of the *Saturday Visitor*, a weekly literary journal of Baltimore, were awarded, by the committee of which he was chairman, to an unknown young man named Poe. It was not deemed proper to give so much to one person, so he received only one prize. It was owing to Mr. Kennedy's interest and kindness that the young author, who was in the most desperate straits, was secured an opening in the columns

95

of the *Southern Literary Messenger* and subsequently became its editor; and the prosperous *littérateur* was the friend and encourager of the indigent genius as long as the latter lived.

Mr. Kennedy's novels, "Swallow Barn," a story of rural life in Virginia; "Horsehoe Robinson," a tale of the Tory ascendency in South Carolina; and "Rob of the Bowl," a story of Maryland, gave him position among the leading novelists of his day, and placed him first among the Southern literary men of his time.

His other works than those named are a satire entitled "Annals of Quodlibet," a memoir of William Wirt, in two volumes, etc. He continued to write until his death, long after the war.

William Gilmore Simms, of South Carolina, was not only the most prolific, but, with the exception of Poe, was the chief distinctly literary man the South has produced. The measure of his industry was immense. His ability was of a high order, and his devotion to literature was, for the time, extraordinary. As a poet, novelist, historian, biographer, essayist, he was not surpassed by any one of his compeers; and if his whole work be considered, he was first. From 1827, when he brought out in Charleston his first venture, a volume entitled "Lyrical and Other Poems,'' to the time of his death in 1870, he was assiduously and earnestly engaged in the attempt to create a literature for the South. His first devotion was to poetry, and he published three volumes of poems before he was twenty-six years of age. Although he continued to write poetry after this, it is chiefly as a writer of fiction that he made his reputation and that his name is now preserved. Poe declared him the best novelist after Cooper this country had produced, and, although to us now his works have the faults of that time, too great prolixity, too much description, and the constant tendency to disquisition, they are of a much higher order as romances than books of many of the novelists of the present day whose works receive general praise. His works comprise a series of novels, most of them based on the more romantic phases of the old Southern life, several volumes of poems, several dramas, and several biographies. ''The Yemassee'' is perhaps the best of his novels, and many of them had a considerable vogue in their day, and the renewed demand for them has recently caused a new edition to be published.

John Esten Cooke, the third of the trio, was like the other two, both a novelist and a biographer. He possessed a fine imagination, and under more exacting conditions he might have reached a high mark and have made a permanent name in our literature. His publications before the war were "Leather Stocking and Silk" (1854), "The Virginia Comedians" (2 vols., 1854), "The Youth of Jefferson" (1854), "Ellie" (1855), "The Last of the Foresters" (1856), and "Bonnybel Vane, or the History of Henry St. John, Gentleman" (1859). In addition to these, he wrote numerous sketches. Candor compels the admission that, although very popular, these earlier works are not of a very high order. The war, however, in which the young novelist served honorably on the staff of General J. E. B. Stuart, the celebrated Confederate cavalry leader, gave him a new impulse, and his later works, such as "Surry of Eagle's Nest," "Mohun," "Hilt to Hilt," "Hammer and Rapier," and "Wearing of the Gray," are very much better than the earlier; whilst his biographical and historical works are probably best of all. These, however, were written under the new conditions, and belong properly to the *post-bellum* literature of the South. Cooke wrote of Virginia life as Simms wrote of South Carolina life, with affection, appreciation, and spirit, but, like both Simms and Kennedy, he failed to strike the highest note. The same may be said of Dr. William A. Caruthers, also a Virginian, who had preceded Cooke and Simms, and who is entitled with the latter and Mr. Kennedy to the honor of first discovering the romantic material afforded the novelist in the picturesque life of their own section. His first book, "The Cavaliers of Virginia, or the Recluse of Jamestown, an Historical Romance of the Old Dominion," appeared in 1832. It dealt with the most romantic episode in the history of the South, if not of the entire country,— Bacon's Rebellion. This was followed in 1854 by the novel on which his name now rests, "The Knights of the Horsehoe, a Traditionary Tale of the Cocked-Hat Gentry in the Old Dominion." He also wrote a volume of sketches entitled "The Kentuckian in New York, or the Adventures of Three Southerners," and a "Life of Dr. Caldwell." This same romantic period was likewise the subject of a novel by St. George Tucker (the younger), entitled "Hansford, a Tale of Bacon's Rebellion," which was published in 1857 by George M. West, of Richmond, Virginia, and which had much popularity in its day.

These books are so good, or, more accurately,

they have in them so much that is good, that one cannot but wonder they are not better. These writers possessed the Southerner's love for the South; they perfectly comprehended the value of the material its life furnished, and recognized the importance of preserving this life in literature; they earnestly endeavored to accomplish this, and yet they failed to preserve it in its reality. It is melancholy to contemplate, and it is difficult to comprehend. They wrote with spirit, with zeal, with affection, and generally in the chastest and most beautiful English, but somehow they just missed the highest mark. It is as if they had set their song in the wrong key.

The chief fault of their books was a certain imitativeness, and adherence to old methods. Scott had set the fashion, and it was so admirable that it led all the writers to copying him. G. P. R. James gave him in dilution. Cooper had attained immense popularity, and was more easily followed; but to imitate Scott was a perilous undertaking. The stripling in the king's armor was not more encumbered.

Yet must this be said in defence of all these writers, that we are looking at their work through a different atmosphere from that in which they wrote. Fashion in writing, where it is not informed by genius, passes away, as in other things. Only art remains ever new, ever fresh, ever true. Just as Miss Burney and Richardson doubtless appeared antiquated to these, so they now appear to us, who are accustomed to a different treatment, stilted and unreal.

After these authors came the sketch-writers, who, if Poe's dictum that a short story is the most perfect form of prose literature is correct, should be placed before them. The chief of these, excepting Poe himself, were Joseph G. Baldwin, Augustus B. Longstreet, William Tappan Thompson, St. Leger L. Carter, and George W. Bagby.

Joseph G. Baldwin was the author of "Flush Times of Alabama and Mississippi," which is perhaps the raciest collection of sketches yet published in America. This volume within a year of its first publication in 1853 had run into its seventh edition. "Ovid Bolus, Esq.," and "Simon Suggs, Jr., Esq.," became at once characters as well known throughout the South as was Sam Weller or Micky Free; whilst the case of "Higginbotham *versus* Swink, Slander," became a *cause célèbre.*

Augustus B. Longstreet, of Mississippi, was

the author of "Georgia Scenes, Characters, Incidents, etc., in the First Half-Century of the Republic," and other sketches. He also wrote a long story entitled "Master William Mitten."

William Tappan Thompson was the author of "Major Jones's Courtship," "Major Jones's Chronicle of Pineville," "Major Jones's Sketches of Travel," and other sketches.

Yet another was Dr. George W. Bagby, of Virginia, who succeeded John R. Thompson as editor of *The Southern Literary Messenger,* and who wrote before the war over the *nom de plume* of "Mozis Addums." The quality of his serious work was higher than that of the other sketch-writers enumerated; and, being wider in its scope, its value was greater than theirs, though his writings were never published in book form until after his death, when two volumes were brought out in Richmond, Virginia. Much of his writing was done after the war, but prior to that period he had accomplished enough to entitle him to the credit of being a literary man at a time when literature in the South was without the compensations by which it was subsequently attended.

No one has ever written so delicately of the South, and his "Old Virginia Gentleman" is the most beautiful sketch of life in the South that has ever appeared.

Besides these classes of writers there existed another class whose writings not only far exceeded in volume those of the authors who have been mentioned, but were also far more successful.

The chief of these were Mrs. Caroline Lee Hentz, Mrs. E. D. E. N. Southworth, Mrs. Catherine Ann Warfield, and Miss Augusta J. Evans. They were followed by a sisterhood of writers far too numerous for mention, whose work, whatever its permanent value, is entitled to honorable notice as evidencing an ambition on the part of the Southern women to create a Southern literature. There were about two hundred in all, who have written novels, books of travel, sketches, and volumes of poems. If they have not generally soared very high, they have at least lifted themselves above the common level, and are entitled to the respect of the South for their loyal endeavor to do their part towards her elevation. Both Mrs. Hentz and Mrs. Southworth wrote many novels and yet more numerous sketches, the popularity of which in their day was extraordinary. Perhaps the best of Mrs. Hentz's romances are "The Mob-Cap" (1848), "Linda" (1850), "Rena" (1851), and "The Planter's Northern Bride." Mrs. Southworth has written over fifty novels, besides shorter stories. Her first book, "Retribution," written for the Washington *National Era*, was subsequently published in a volume in 1849, and had an immense sale. It was rapidly followed by "The Deserted Wife," "The Missing Bride," "Love's Labor Won," "The Lost Heiress," "Fallen Pride," "Curse of Clifton," etc., to the number above stated. In all of these novels the element of romance is emphasized. Some of Mrs. Southworth's books were vehemently assailed, but, as the public is much more intent on being entertained than on being elevated, they generally attained an extensive popularity. The Southern life is utilized by both these writers, but in so exaggerated or unreal a form that the pictures are too untrue to be relied on. Both authors were of Northern birth, whilst their lives were spent at the South. Is it significant of the fact that the Northern literary press was not in "old times" open to writers of Southern birth, or that public sentiment was against Southern women publishing, or of both?

Mrs Terhune ("Marion Harland") is entitled to stand in a class by herself, since her books "Alone," "The Hidden Path," "Mossside," and "Nemesis," which were published before the war, as well as those which have appeared since that time, are in a much higher literary key than those of the authors named. Like the others, she has used the Southern life as material in her work; but she has exhibited a literary sense of a far higher order, and an artistic touch to which the others are strangers.

There existed yet another class, whose work, although not extensive in amount, was yet of a quality to enlist the attention and evoke the respect of American readers. The Southern poets were not numerous: poetry even more peculiarly than prose demands a sympathetic atmosphere. Such was not to be found at the South. The standards there were Shakespeare, Dryden, and Pope; no less would be tolerated. Before Wilde could admit his authorship of "My Life is like the Summer Rose" he had to establish himself as a fine lawyer and an able politician; Philip Pendleton Cooke, as an offset to "Florence Vane" and the "Froissart Ballads," found it necessary to avouch his manhood as the crack turkey-shot of the Valley of Virginia. Yet the poets wrote, if not much, still real poetry, and poetry which will live as a part of the best American literature. In this domain, as in others, Poe soared high above all the rest. He was not profuse; but he was excellent, pre-eminent. He is one of the poets of the English-speaking race. Wilde, Cooke, Pinkney, Key, Meek, Lamar, Lipscomb, Vawter, and others have been already referred to. The "Sonnet to a Mockingbird" by the first is as fine as his other more popular poem already mentioned. Mr. Wilde resided in Italy for some time, and published the result of his researches there in a work in two volumes, entitled "Conjectures and Researches concerning the Love, Madness, and Imprisonment of Torquato Tasso," which contains fine translations from Tasso and is otherwise valuable. He also wrote a "Life of Dante," and a long poem entitled "Hesperia," besides a number of translations of Italian lyrics which were not published until after his death.

Cooke, besides "Florence Vane," which Poe declared the sweetest lyric ever written in America, and which has been translated into many foreign languages, wrote many other lyrics, of which the most popular and perhaps the best are the "Lines to my Daughter Lily" and "Rosa Lee." He also wrote a number of sketches, among which are "John Carpe," "The Gregories of Hackwood," and "The Crime of Andrew Blair."

He died at the age of thirty-three, when his brilliant powers were still in bud.

Edward Coate Pinkney was a member of a family distinguished for literary taste and ability. His uncle, Ninian Pinkney, as early as 1809 published a book of "Travels in the South of France and in the Interior of the Provinces of Provence and Languedoc," of which Leigh Hunt said, "It set all the idle world to going to France to live on the charming banks of the Loire."

His brother Frederick was also a poet. Pinkney's poems were so exquisite that after their first publication in 1825 he was requested to sit for a portrait to be included in a sketch of "The Five Greatest Poets of the Nation." "A Health" and "The Picture Song" have an established place in our literature.

Lanier and Ticknor, of Georgia; John R. Thompson, of Virginia; Dimitry, of Louisiana; Ryan, etc., belong to a later time. Sidney Lanier was easily the next Southern poet to Poe, and has not been surpassed by any other that this country has produced.

Perhaps Henry Timrod and Paul H. Hayne also more properly belong to that period, but before the war they had done work which by its worth and volume entitles them to be ranked of all Southern poets next after Poe.

Hayne in South Carolina was, with Simms and others, inspiring just before the war an emulation which promised a brighter literary future than there had previously been ground to hope for. John R. Thompson, as editor of the *Southern Literary Messenger,* was performing the same work for Virginia. Had Hayne and Thompson received greater encouragement, their fine talents might have yielded a return which would have made their native land as proud of her brilliant sons as they deserved.

Besides the authors mentioned in this paper, there were very many others who, by occasional essays at literature in prose or in verse, attained something more than a local reputation, but they were distinguished rather in other professions than in literature, whilst most of those which have been mentioned are now chiefly distinguished for the literary work they accomplished.

If it shall appear from this very imperfect summary of the literary work done by the South, and of the causes which influenced it, that the amount produced was small, attention should be called again first, to the insignificant number of the slave-holding whites of the South, from whom alone, as the educated class, a literature could come; and secondly, to the intellectual energy which that limited population displayed throughout the entire period of their existence. The intellectual work they accomplished will compare not unfavorably with that of a similar number of any other people during the same period; and the thoughtful and dispassionate student, to whatever causes he may deem to be due the absence of a literature among the Southern people, will not attribute it to either mental indigence or mental lassitude.

GLIMPSES OF LIFE IN COLONIAL VIRGINIA

GLIMPSES OF LIFE IN
COLONIAL VIRGINIA

FEW things relating to the South have been more misunderstood than its social life. Even the Southern people themselves have not generally had a very correct idea of its proportions.

Owing to the astounding indifference of our people to the preservation of records; to the extraordinary environment in which they were placed; to the wonderful rapidity with which the country advanced in its development, ever pushing its confines further and further before the interior could be filled in, there are scarcely any written records of our life remaining extant. Few letters, journals, or accounts have been published or even preserved, and the records to which writers have gone for their materials are almost exclusively the impressions of temporary sojourners, who at one time or another have passed hastily through our borders, generally without either the opportunity or the capacity to form other than a hasty or prejudiced opinion.

The Southern civilization was in its character as distinctive as was that of Greece, Carthage, Rome, or Venice. It has had no chronicler to tell its story in that spirit of sympathy from which alone can come the lights and shadings on which depend perspective and real truth.

It deserves such a recorder, for it produced results the consequences of which may never cease. Among them is this nation.

The social life of a people embraces their daily life in their homes, with all that relates to their social customs and intercourse. It is at once the occasion and the reflection of the character of the people. Whatever may throw light on these is relevant to the subject.

It is, therefore, pertinent to investigate the causes which contributed to any distinctive form which that life may have taken, to show that peculiar form itself, and to touch upon the results it produced.

The structure of that life was, in the first place, consequent upon the origin of the people, the manner in which they were planted here, and the conditions of their existence; whilst the continuance of the institution of domestic slavery constituted a potent force in giving to it its distinctive character.

The shadow of this institution appears to have fallen upon it, and to have prevented a wholly just and proper view of its true character.

But though it is impossible to do more in a single paper than simply suggest the outline of the complete picture, yet the attempt will be made to draw that outline in the hope that some abler artist may one day give the world the very lines and spirit of what is believed by some to have been the sweetest, purest, and most beautiful life ever lived.

And first, as to its origin.

Long before any English colony was permanently established on these shores, England, in envy of Spain, was looking about to assert a claim to a part of the new world, the wealth of which was so fabulous.

The first charter to John Cabot, in 1496, confined his discoveries to the region north of 44° N. latitude, recognizing Spain's right, as fixed by the Pope, to all that might lie south of that degree. Edward VI, being Protestant, his charter to the "merchant adventurers" did not regard these bounds. Mary, however, shackled by religious bigotry and the influence of Philip, restrained the growing enterprise of her subjects, and humbly submitting to the Pope's decrees, once more yielded to Spain all that country claimed. Elizabeth was of different stuff. She flung down the gauntlet. Her first Parliament vested in her the supremacy claimed by the Pope, with all that it implied. From this time America became the prize between Roman Catholicism and Protestantism. In 1562 Admiral Coligny attempted to establish a Huguenot colony in South Carolina, and two years later he settled a small colony in Florida, where most of his colonists were subsequently killed by the Spaniards. Captain John Hawkins, under the patronage of the Earl of Pembroke, Lord Robert Dudley, Sir William Cecil, and other nobles, voyaged to the South and made explorations. This Spain would not endure. In 1568 Hawkins, then on his third voyage, met and had a great sea fight with the Spaniards off Vera Cruz, in which he lost three of his ships. He was forced to put ashore one hundred and fourteen of his men, several of whom marched north along the coast. The Spaniards caught most of those who remained, sentenced sixty-eight of them to the galleys, and burnt three of them,—America's first *auto da fé.*

Reports of the fabulous wealth of this Southern land had spread in England. The merchant adventurers had long been watching the stream of wealth pouring through the plate galleons into Spain. They had got an act passed extending their privileges and setting forth their object "for the discovery of new trades." The prize was coveted by others than the merchants, and the new land was claimed as "fatally reserved for England." Sir Philip Sidney, in the summer of 1584, began to take an interest in American enterprises. He was interested in Raleigh's voyage, but projected an expedition under the command of Sir Francis Drake and himself, a scheme which Fulke Greville says "was the exactest model Europe ever saw, a conquest not to be enterprised but by Sir Philip's reaching spirit that grasped all circumstances and interests."

Elizabeth had taken into her favor a young man who even in that adventurous age had displayed extraordinary qualities, a young Devonshire gentleman, described by an old chroni-

cler as "of a good presence in a well-compacted
body, strong, natural wit and better judgment,
a bold and plausible tongue, the fancy of a
poet, and the chivalry of a soldier." He was
cousin to Sir Richard Grenville, who brought
undying fame to our race when with the little
Revenge he fought the Spaniard at Flores,
and he was half-brother to those bold, adventurous navigators, Sir Humphrey, Sir John,
and Sir Adrian Gilbert, who with him did
more than any other family to wrest this continent from Spain and make it an "English
nation." Dashing soldier as he was, queller
of rebellions, patron of poets, stout hater and
fighter of Spain, "admiral and shepherd of
the ocean," it was his highest title that he was
"Lord and Chief Governor of Virginia." It
is likewise one of Virginia's chief glories that
she owes her name and her being, at least in
its peculiar form, to the stout, high-minded,
and chivalric soldier, the most picturesque
character in modern history,—second in his
work only to Christopher Columbus,—Sir
Walter Raleigh.

Although the colonies which Raleigh planted
perished, his mighty enterprise laid the foundation for the final establishment of Virginia,

and his spirit fixed its imperishable impress upon the work and gave it its distinctive character. He was at Oxford when England thrilled with the news of Hawkins's third voyage. He left the University to fight the Spaniard in the low country. From that time Spain was his quarry. He spent his great life in wresting America from her hands. He awakened in England an interest in the new land which never died out; made its holding a matter of national pride and national principle; excited British pride and religious fervor; stimulated the flagging, awakened public enthusiasm; aroused the Church, and created the spirit which, in spite of numberless disasters and repeated failures, finally verified his high prophecy to Sir Robert Cecil, that he would "live to see Virginia an English nation."

The names of the men who engaged in these enterprises are enough to show how the aristocratic character became fixed on the Southern settlement. The South was settled not merely under the patronage of, but largely by, the better class in England. The queen sent Sir Humphrey Gilbert an anchor set with jewels, and a message that she "wished him as great hap and safety to his ship as if she herself were there in person."

Raleigh's high spirit gave the colony a priceless benefaction. He obtained in his charter (of 1584) a provision that his colonists should "have all the privileges of free denizens and natives of England, and were to be governed according to such statutes as should by them be established, so that the said statutes or laws conform as conveniently as may be with those of England," etc.

These guaranties were the rock on which the American people founded their impregnable claim to those rights which are now deemed inherent and inalienable. They bore an important part in the social as well as the political life of the people. They were renewed in the charter of 1606 under which the colony came which finally secured in Virginia a lasting foothold, and established here the rule of the Anglo-Saxon race. They were never forgot by the stout adventurers who came to endure the hardships of the New World, "leaving their bodies in testimonie of their minds."

They formed the foundation of that pride and independence which became so notable a characteristic of the social life and gave it its individuality.

For many years daring young members of the great families with their retainers had been going abroad, taking service in the Low Countries, and feeding their instinct for adventure. The wars were now over; London was filled with these soldiers, without means and with the wandering habit strong on them, brave to recklessness, without steady habits of industry, ready for any adventure. Filled with the enthusiasm of exploration and colonization, fired by the tales of the Gilberts, of Grenville, Hawkins, Gosnold, Stukeley, and others, the colonizing spirit of the English race found here a field; and Virginia became the El Dorado of the British nation.

Thus Virginia was settled with a strong English feeling ingrained in her, with English customs and habits of life, with English ideas modified only to suit the conditions of existence here.

Among the chief factors which influenced the Virginia life and moulded it in its peculiar form were this English feeling (which was almost strong enough to be termed a race feeling); the aristocratic tendency; the happy combination of soil, climate and agricultural product (tobacco), which made them an agricultural people, and enabled them to support a generous style of living as landed gentry; the Church with its strong organization; and the institution of slavery.

The fabulous reports of Virginia's wealth, so well known that it was travestied upon the stage as a land where the pots and pans and the very chains that bound the slaves were of gold, and jewels of marvellous value were picked up on the seashore to adorn the savage children, undoubtedly at first induced many adventurers to come to Virginia who had no thought of remaining longer than was necessary to make fortunes which they proposed to spend in England. These were followed by others who wished not to sever altogether their old ties, and for many years life here must have been intolerably hard to those accustomed to the pleasant paths of old England. Thus England for several generations was to the Virginians "home."

The commerce with her through the ports of the Chesapeake was direct, vessels loading with tobacco from the warehouses of the planters on the rivers. "Every person may, with ease, procure a small plantation, can ship his tobacco at his own door, and live independent,'' says the English traveller Burnaby.

This proved a strong and ever fresh bond, preserving as it did immediate and constant intercourse between the new country and the old.

The land-holding instinct of the people displayed itself from the first, and they settled large plantations along the rivers, where the fertility of the soil enabled them to raise tobacco, and the waterways afforded them means to ship. Here they set up establishments as nearly like those of the landed gentry of England as the conditions of the new land admitted.

The existence of African slaves brought in by Dutch, English, and New England traders, and the exportation from England of persons who were sold as indented servants, enabled the Virginians to cultivate their lands, and gave them the means to support their pretensions as a landed gentry. The institution of slavery was a potent factor. In the beginning it was slow in its growth.

The first cargo were but 20, who were brought in a Dutch ship, which put into Hampton Roads in 1619. In 1749 there were but 300 in the colony. The first American slaver, *The Desire*, had, however, been fitted out at Salem in 1636, and others followed, and in 1670 there were 2000 negroes in the colony; in 1714 there were but 23,000, and in 1756, 120,000, 52,000 more being in the other colonies, including New England.

The existence of slaves emphasized the class distinction and created a system of castes, making the social system of Virginia as strongly aristocratic as that in England.

The law itself recognized the distinction of class. "Such persons of quality," says an act of 1835-36, "as shall be found delinquent in their duties, being not fitt to undergoe corporal punishment, may notwithstanding be ymprisoned at the discretion of ye commander." The governor was empowered to "presse men of the ordinary sort" to work on the State House, paying of course proper wages in tobacco.

There were no titles save the "Honourables" of the counsellors, the "Esquires," and the "Colonels," who commanded in the various counties.

Titles could have added nothing to their distinction. They erected their brick mansions on the hills above the rivers, flanked by their offices and out-buildings, placed their negro quarters conveniently behind them, and ruled in a system as manorial as that in the old country.

The royal governors aided this aristocratic tendency. Many of them were men of rank at home, and when they came over they set up in the Province a court as nearly vice-regal as their circumstances admitted. The House of Burgesses was like the House of Commons, and was composed of men of any class. The King's Council of twelve having the powers of a general court, besides possessing certain executive powers, was appointed, and came insensibly to be a "miniature House of Lords," untitled and not hereditary it is true, but yet practically controlled by the great planter families.

The English system of primogeniture and of entail prevailed in as rigid a form as in the old country. The fostering sympathy of the Church bore its fruit; and the established Church at home became naturally the estab-lished Church in Virginia, a law being passed by the General Assembly (1624-32) that the colony is to conform "both in canons and con-stitution to the Church of England as near as may be." "They made many laws against the Puritans, though they were free from them," writes the Rev. Hugh Jones in his "Present State of Virginia," p. 23. Both "Papists" and "Puritans" were dealt with vigorously, being driven out either to Maryland or New England; and non-conformists were held to strict compliance with the law.

Undoubtedly many, both at first and later on, came to Virginia who were not of gentle birth; but the lines were too clearly drawn to admit of confusion; those who possessed the personal force requisite, rose and were absorbed into the upper class; but the great body of them remained a class distinct from this. In the contest between Charles I and his Parliament, the people of Virginia, following their instincts, at the final rupture sided overwhelmingly with the king, and Virginia had become so well recognized as an aristocratic country that after the failure of the Royalist arms, there was a notable emigration of followers of the king to the colony, which, under the stout old Cavalier governor, Sir William Berkeley, had been unswerving in its loyalty. When the king was beheaded, the House of Burgesses gave expression to the general horror. One of the first acts, if not the very first, speaks of him as "The late, most excellent, and now undoubtedly sainted King," and provides that "what person soever shall go about to defend or maintain the late traitorous proceedings against the aforesaid King of most happy memory shall be adjudged an accessory, post-factum to the death of the aforesaid King, and shall be proceeded against for the same, according to the known laws of England."

Holding true to the crown the Virginians, when Charles II was a fugitive in Holland, sent commissioners to offer him an unlapsed kingdom beyond the seas, and, according to Jones, she was the last to acknowledge Cromwell and the first to proclaim king Charles II even before the Restoration ("Present State of Virginia," p. 23).

Yet there was that in the Virginians which distinguished them, for all their aristocratic pretensions, from their British cousins. Grafted on the aristocratic instinct was a jealous watchfulness of their liberties, a guardfulness of their rights, which developed into a sterling republicanism, notwithstanding the aristocratic instinct. The standard was not birth nor family connection; it was one based on individual attainment.

Sir Walter Raleigh had obtained a guarantee of British rights in his charter. Sir Francis Wyatt had brought over in 1622 a charter with an extension of these rights. The General Assembly, convened in 1619 when there were only eleven boroughs, jealously guarded their liberties. They refused to give their records for inspection to the royal commissioners, and when their clerk disobeyed them and gave them up, they cut off one of his ears and put him in the pillory. They passed statutes limiting the power of the governor to lay taxes only through the General Assembly.

When Charles I, for whom they were ready to vote or fight, claimed a monopoly of the tobacco trade, the royal people of Virginia protested with a vigor which brought him to a stand; when Cromwell sent his governor, they deposed him and immediately re-elected him that he might act only by their authority. They offered Charles II a kingdom; but when he granted the Northern Neck to Culpepper and Arlington they grew ready for revolution.

Many of the best known of the older families of Virginia are descended from royalist refugees.

On the Restoration some of the adherents of the Commonwealth, finding England too hot for them, came over; but they were held in no very high general esteem, and the old order continued to prevail.

The spirit of the colony will appear from the following act, which was adopted 18th March, 1660-61: "Whereas our late surrender and submission to that execrable power, that soe bloodyly massacred the late King Charles I of blessed [in a revision is added, "and glorious"] memory, hath made us, by acknowledging them guilty of their crimes, to show our serious and hearty repentance and detestation of that barbarous act, *Bee* itt enacted that the 30th of January, the day the said King was beheaded, be annually solemnized with fasting and prayers that our sorrowes may expiate our crime and our teares wash away our guilt" (Hen. Vol. 11, p. 24).

As the eighteenth century passed, the settlement pushed further and further westward. A new element came in by way of the upper valley of Virginia, stout Scotch-Irish Presbyterian settlers, from Scotland first, and then from Ireland, with the colonizing spirit strong in them; simple in their life, stern in their faith, dauntless in their courage, a race to found and to hold new lands against all comers or claimants; a race whose spirit was more potent than the line of forts with which the French attempted to hem them in along the Belle Rivière. They founded a new colony looking to the West and the new land, as the old planter settlers towards the sea looked to the East and the old.

Burnaby, the traveller already quoted, paid a visit to the valley in which they had first made their home. "I could not but reflect with pleasure on the situation of these people," says he, "and think if there is such a thing as happiness in this life that they enjoy it. Far from the bustle of the world, they live in the most delightful climate and richest soil imaginable; they are everywhere surrounded with beautiful prospects and sylvan scenes; lofty mountains, transparent streams, falls of water, rich valleys, and majestic woods; the whole interspersed with an infinite variety of flowering shrubs, constitute the landscape surrounding them. . . . They live in perfect liberty, they are ignorant of want and acquainted with but few vices. . . . They possess what many princes would give half their dominions for, health, content, and tranquillity of mind."

Now and then the lines crossed, and, with

intercourse, gradually the aristocratic tendency of the seaboard and Piedmont became grafted into the patriarchal system of the valley, distinctly coloring it, though the absence of slaves in numbers softened the lines marking the class-distinctions.

The lands were sometimes held on a feudal tenure. William Byrd held and let his lands at the Falls of James on a feudal tenure.

"And he shall become bound and obliged," runs the grant, "to seat the whole number of fifty able men armed and constantly furnished with sufficient ammunition and provisions together with such number of tithable persons, not exceeding 250 in the whole on both sides of said River," etc.

On this spot now stands Richmond, which in the great civil war was for four years the point of attack by the Northern armies.

A similar grant on the Rappahannock River was made to Lawrence Smith, and was offered to any other persons at, or near, the heads of any other of the great rivers, on condition of their placing there military forces and other persons "for the protection of his Majesty's country against our barbarous enemy, the Indians."

Indeed, the wealthy planter families from

the rivers, holding their places in council generation after generation, and ever spreading out more and more, maintained a system as nearly a copy of that in England when they came over, as the conditions of the new land admitted.

The royal governor occupied, in the capital city, a mansion called the "Palace," and during the sessions of the Assembly the gentlefolk of the colony assembled at Williamsburg, and "the season" was celebrated as distinctly as it was in London during the sitting of Parliament.

Here is a picture of the capital: "There is one handsome street in it, just a mile in length, with the capitol on one side of the street; and the college of William and Mary, an old monastic structure, at the other end. About the middle between them on the north side, a little distance retired from the street, stands the palace, the residence of the governor; a large, commodious and handsome building."

"Here dwell several good families," says the Rev. Hugh Jones, who had lived among them, "and more reside here in their own houses at public times. They live in the same neat manner, dress after the same modes, and behave themselves exactly as the gentry in London. Most families of any note having a coach, chariot, berlin, or chaise.''

The people being almost universally agricultural, and there being no cities and no great difference of interests, the structure of society was naturally simple.

The African slaves formed by position and race the lowest stratum. Next to them were the indented servants, and the lowest class of whites, composed of indented servants and the worst element of the transported whites, called in Virginia ''jail birds,'' who were shipped from the cities of England, and who although as absolutely under the dominion of their masters during the period of servitude as the slaves themselves, yet in virtue of their race potentiality had rights denied to the slaves, and possessed the future, if not the present. Next were the small farmers and new-comers of modest means, who were continually increasing in numbers and who were ever striving to rise, and some of them successfully, in the social scale. Finally, over all was the upper class: the large planters and shippers, who owned extensive lands and many slaves; lived in the style of country gentlemen of means;

jealously guarded their privileges, and as counsellors, commissioners, and colonels managed the colony as if it had been their private estate.

"There is a greater distinction supported between the different classes of life here than perhaps in any of the rest of the colonies," says the English traveller, Smythe, "nor does that spirit of equality and levelling principle which pervades the greater part of America prevail to such an extent in Virginia.

"However, there appear to be but three degrees of rank amongst all the inhabitants exclusive of the negroes.

"The first consists of gentlemen of the best families and fortunes of the colony, who are here much more respectable and numerous than in any other province in America. These, in general, have had a liberal education, possess enlightened understandings, and a thorough knowledge of the world, that furnishes them with an ease and freedom of manners and conversation highly to their advantage in exterior, which no vicissitude of fortune or place can divest them of; they being actually, according to my ideas, the most agreeable and best companions, friends, and neighbors that need be desired.

"The greater number of them keep their carriages and have handsome services of plate; but they all without exception have studs, as well as sets of elegant and beautiful horses.

"Those of the second degree in rank are very numerous, being perhaps half the inhabitants, and consists of such a variety, singularity, and mixture of characters that the exact general criterion and leading feature can scarcely be ascertained.

"However, they are generous, friendly, and hospitable in the extreme; but mixed with such an appearance of rudeness, ferocity, and haughtiness, which is in fact only a want of polish, occasioned by their deficiencies in education and a knowledge of mankind, as well as by their general intercourse with slaves."

Many of these possessed fortunes superior to some of the first rank, "but" says Smythe, "their families are not so ancient nor respectable; a circumstance here held in some estimation."

"They are all," he adds, "excessively attached to every species of sport, gaming, and dissipation, particularly horse-racing, and that most barbarous of all diversions, that peculiar species of cruelty, cock-fighting.

"Numbers of them are truly valuable members of society, and few or none deficient in the excellencies of the intellectual faculties, and a natural genius which, though in a great measure unimproved, is generally bright and splendid in an uncommon degree.

"The third, or lower class of the people (who ever compose the bulk of mankind), are in Virginia more few in number in proportion to the rest of the inhabitants than perhaps in any other country in the Universe. Even these are kind, hospitable, and generous; yet illiberal, noisy, and rude. They are much addicted to inebriety, and averse to labor.

"They are likewise overburdened with an impertinent and insuperable curiosity, that renders them peculiarly disagreeable and troublesome to strangers."

This is a strong indictment against "the third or lower class" to whom it is confined in Virginia, but our traveller seems not to have found this peculiar to the Virginia poor whites, for he immediately adds:

"Yet these undesirable qualities they possess by no means in an equal degree with the generality of the inhabitants of New England, whose religion and government have encouraged, and indeed instituted and established, a kind of inquisition of forward impertinence and prying intrusion against every person that may be compelled to pass through that troublesome, illiberal country; from which description, however, there are no doubt many exceptions.''

On the whole, this is apparently not an inaccurate analysis of the character of the good people of Virginia at that time, as they lived their easy, contented, careless lives on their plantations or farms, in their orchard-embowered homes. The slaves were multiplying rapidly. The laws devised to regulate them may appear to this humanitarian generation very harsh, but most of them were savages fresh from the wilds of Africa; and, at least, the laws were no severer than those enacted in Massachusetts and other colonies. In practical operation this severity was tempered by the friendliness which sprang up between the slaves and their masters, the relation between them invariably becoming a sort of feudal one, and the slaves living happy and contented lives. This appears to have been a continual puzzle to the outsiders who visited the colony. Smythe, the same traveller quoted, after speaking with astonishment of the laws provided for their regulation, and expressing great commiseration over their condition, declares:

"Yet notwithstanding this degraded situation, and rigid severity to which fate has subjected this wretched race, they are certainly devoid of care, and actually appear jovial, contented, and happy."

He can scarcely credit his senses; he records with astonishment the fact that after the "severe labor" which he asserts continues for "some hours" after dusk, "instead of retiring to rest as might naturally be concluded he would be glad to do, he generally sets out from home, and walks six or seven miles in the night, be the weather ever so sultry, to a negroe dance in which he performs with astonishing agility, and the most vigorous exertions, keeping time and cadence most exactly, with the music of the banjor, a large hollow instrument with three strings, and a quaqua (somewhat resembling a drum), until he exhausts himself, and has scarcely time or strength to return home before the time he is called forth to toil next morning."

All his pity for the negroes, however, did not prevent his purchasing one for forty pounds, along with two horses to continue his

journey to North Carolina. In view of his abhorrence of slavery, it would be interesting to
know what became of this boy afterwards.

Slavery in any form shocks the sensibilities
of this age; but surely this banjo-playing life
was not so dreadful a lot for those just rescued
from the cannibalism of the Congo.

The relation between the poor whites and
the upper classes was not so intimate as that
between the slaves and their masters, and the
former lived very much as the lower peasantry
do in all countries, standing somewhat in the
relation of retainers of or dependents on the
planter class.

The distinction between the middle class, or
small farmers, and the wealthier planters was
very clearly marked up to the Revolution, at
which time the diffusion of the planter families had greatly increased the number of lesser
planters of good family connection, and the
common defence of all the country opened the
path of distinction to all, irrespective of social
station.

The planters lived in a style patterned on
that of the landed gentry in England, maintaining large establishments on their plantations, surrounded by slaves and servants, dis-

pensing a prodigal hospitality, wearing silks and velvets imported from abroad, expending their incomes, and often more than their incomes, engaging in horse-racing and other gentle diversions, and generally arrogating to themselves all the privileges of an exclusive upper class. "At the governor's house upon birth nights and at balls and assemblies," says the Rev. Hugh Jones in his "Present State of Virginia," "I have seen as fine an appearance, as good diversion, and as splendid entertainment in Governor Spotswood's time as I have seen anywhere else."

They built churches, reserving pews in the chancels or galleries like the Lords of the Manors in England. The Carters built a church at Corotoman, and the congregation waited respectfully outside till the family arrived and entered, when they followed them in. The Wormleys, the Grymeses, the Churchills, and the Berkeleys built an addition to the church in Middlesex for their exclusive use. Mr. Matthew Kemp, as church warden, received the commendation of the vestry in the same county for displacing an unworthy woman who insisted on taking a pew above her degree.

One old grand dame at her death had herself buried under the transept used by the poor, that in punishment for her pride they might trample upon her grave.

The mansions of this class were. generally set back in groves of forest trees upon the heights overlooking the rivers, and were heavy and roomy brick structures flanked by "offices." They were substantial rather than showy, though their very simplicity was often impressive. Many specimens of the kind still remain, though in a state of sad decay, on the James, the York, and the Rappahannock rivers. The houses of the middle classes were generally of wood.

Here are bits of description from Smythe's "Travels."

"On the 6th," he says, "the ship weighed anchor and proceeded up James River. . . . After passing a great number of most charming situations on each side of this beautiful river, we came to anchor.

"The principal situations that commanded my notice and admiration were Shirley Hundred, a seat of Charles Carter, Esq., at present in the occupation of Mr. Bowler Cock; this is, indeed, a charming place; the buildings are of brick, large, convenient, and expensive, but now falling to decay; they were erected at a great charge by Mr Carter's father, who was secretary of the colony, and this was his favorite seat of residence. The present proprietor has a most opulent fortune, and possesses such a variety of seats in situations so extremely delightful, that he overlooks this sweet one of Shirley and suffers it to fall into ruin, although the buildings must have cost an immense sum in constructing, and would certainly be expensive to keep in repair." Arrived at the Falls where now stands Richmond, then a collection of small villages, he, after speaking of its situation, bursts forth, filled with admiration at the beauty of the land:

"Whilst the mind is filled with astonishment and novel objects, all the senses are gratified.

"The flowering shrubs which overspread the land regale the smell with odoriferous perfumes; and fruits of exquisite relish and flavor delight the taste and afford a most grateful refreshment."

As the tide of settlement rolled westward, simple wooden houses were often built by the slaves, of timber, cut and sawed by hand upon the place, to which wings were added for convenience, as the family increased. There was not generally much display in the buildings themselves, the extravagance being reserved for the cheer dispensed within. The furniture, however, was often elaborate and handsome, being imported from England, and generally of the finest wood, such as mahogany and rose-wood. Chariots and four were the ordinary mode of travel, the difficulties of country roads giving the gentry a reasonable excuse for gratifying their pride in this respect.

Their love of fine horses very early displayed itself, and laws were enacted at an early time for improving the strain of their blood in Virginia. "They are such lovers of riding," says the Rev. Mr. Jones, in his "Present State of Virnigia," "that almost every ordinary person keeps a horse, and I have known some spend the morning in ranging several miles in the woods to find and catch their horses only to ride two or three miles to church, to the court-house, or to a horse-race."

"The horses are fleet and beautiful," says Burnaby, "and the gentlemen of Virginia, who are exceedingly fond of horse-racing, have spared no expense or trouble to improve the breed of these by importing great numbers from England."

143

Each spring and fall there were races at Williamsburg, where two, three, and four mile heats were run for purses as high as a hundred pounds, besides matches and sweepstakes for considerable sums, "the inhabitants almost to a man being quite devoted to the diversion of horse-racing." "Very capital horses are started here," says the traveller Smythe, "such as would make no despicable figure at New-market; nor is their speed, bottom, or blood inferior to their appearance, the gentlemen of Virginia sparing no pains, trouble, or expense in importing the best stock and improving the excellence of the breed by proper and judicious crossing. Indeed nothing can be more elegant and beautiful than the horses bred here, either for the turf, the field, the road, or the coach."

"Virginians," he adds, "of all ranks and denominations are excessively fond of horses and especially those of the race breed. The gentlemen of fortune expend great sums on their studs, generally keeping handsome carriages and several sets of horses, as well as others for the race and road; even the most indigent person has his saddle horse, which he rides to every place and on every occasion; for in this country nobody walks on foot the smallest distance except when hunting.'' He, too, observes that ''a man will frequently go five miles to catch a horse, to ride only one mile upon afterwards.''

The traveller knew something of Virginia life.

The Rev. Andrew Burnaby, rector of Greenwich, where he confines himself to what he saw, is picturesque and reliable; when he does not, he is simply picturesque. Virginians struck him as ''indolent, easy, and good-natured, extremely fond of society, and much given to convivial pleasures.'' In consequence of this, charges Burnaby, ''they seldom show any spirit of enterprise or expose themselves to fatigue.'' They were, he thought, ''vain and imperious and entire strangers to that elegance of sentiment which is so peculiarly characteristic of refined and polished nations.'' He has the grace to admit that ''general characters are always liable to many exceptions. In Virginia I have had the pleasure to know several gentlemen adorned with many virtues and accomplishments to whom the following description is by no means applicable.''

As to this absence of refined feeling, we shall see presently.

"The public or political character of the Virginians," he says, "corresponds with their private one; they are haughty and jealous of their liberties, impatient of restraint, and can scarcely bear the thought of being controlled by any superior power. Many of them consider the colonies as independent States, not connected with Great Britain, otherwise than by having the same common King, and being bound to her with natural affection."

Perhaps this independence was not agreeable to the reverend rector of Greenwich's loyal instincts.

He was not so accurate in his observations on the private character of the Virginians as on their political. He noted that they never refuse any necessary supplies for the support of the government when called upon, and are a generous and loyal people.

Here is what he says of the Virginia women: "The women are, upon the whole, rather handsome, but not to be compared with our fair country women in England. [He was writing for publication in England.] They have but few advantages and consequently are seldom accomplished; this makes them reserved and unequal to any interesting and refined con-

146

versation. They are immoderately fond of dancing, and indeed it is almost the only amusement they partake of." He then describes the country dances and "jijjs" they dance, which may give an idea of the society in which he generally moved.

(The Rev. Hugh Jones in his "Present State of Virginia" sufficiently discriminates the two classes of society with their diversions to show that although the English traveller mentioned may have occasionally been entertained at a gentleman's house, yet the people whom he described belonged unquestionably to the second class.)

"The Virginia ladies," he proceeds, "excepting these amusements and now and then a party of pleasure into the woods to partake of a barbecue, chiefly spend their time in sewing and taking care of their families. They seldom read or endeavor to improve their minds; however, they are in general good housewives, and though they have not, I think, quite as much tenderness and sensibility as the English ladies, yet they make as good wives and as good mothers as any in the world."

It is surprising that he should have passed so general a stricture on the lack of enterprise of the Virginians, for he records the famous feat of Washington in going with a single companion to the "Ohio River" with letters to the French commander, M. St. Pierre, in 1753, but a few years before, and he certainly did not underestimate the act.

The distance was more than four hundred miles, two hundred of which lay through a trackless forest inhabited by treacherous and merciless savages, and the season was unusually severe.

It was less than fifteen years after this that these Virginians, with a mightiness of enterprise which must have shaken the reverend traveller's confidence in his judgment, helped to build a nation and tear from England the richest possession any country ever owned.

The hospitality of the good people of the colony early became noted, and its exercise was so unstinted, so universal, so cordial, that it has acquired for itself the honor of a special designation, and, the world over, has set the standard as "Virginia hospitality."

"They shall be reputed to entertain those of curtesie with whom they make not a certaine agreement," says the old Statute of 1661-62 (Hen. 1661-62, 1667).

148

Here is what the traveller Smythe says of his experience in this regard: "The Virginians are generous, extremely hospitable, and possess very liberal sentiments. . . . To communicate an idea of the general hospitality that prevails in Virginia, and, indeed, throughout all the Southern provinces, it may not be improper to represent some peculiar customs that are universal; for instance:

"If a traveller, even a negro, observes an orchard full of fine fruit, either apples or peaches, in or near his way, he alights without ceremony, and fills his pockets, or even a bag, if he has one, without asking permission; and if the proprietor should see him, he is not in the least offended, but makes him perfectly welcome, and assists him in choosing out the finest fruit." He explains that this was not to be wondered at as fruit was so plentiful that peaches were fed to the hogs; and proceeds: "When a person of more genteel figure than common calls at an ordinary (the name of their inns), for refreshment and lodging for a night, as soon as any of the gentlemen of fortune in the neighborhood hears of it, he either comes for him himself, or sends him a polite and pressing invitation to his home, where he meets with entertainment and accommodation infinitely superior in every respect to what he could have received at the inn. If he should happen to be fatigued with travelling, he is treated in the most hospitable and genteel manner, and his servants and horses also fare plenteously, for as long a time as he chooses to stay. All this is done with the best grace imaginable, without even a hint being thrown out of a curiosity or wish to know his name.''

Are these the people that Parson Burnaby says are ''entire strangers to that elegance of sentiment which is so peculiarly characteristic of refined and polished nations''?

If you would have a picture of a country family of that time, here is one by the Chevalier de Chastellux, who was a Major-General under Rochambeau in the Revolutionary Army, and who wrote an account of his travels in Virginia in 1780-82. He relates a visit he paid General Nelson's family at Offley, an unpretentious country place in Hanover County. He says:

''In the absence of the General (who had gone to Williamsburg) his mother and wife received us with all the politeness, ease, and cordiality natural to his family. But, as in America, the ladies are never thought sufficient to do

the honors of the house, five or six Nelsons
were assembled to receive us, among others:
Secretary Nelson, uncle to the General, his two
sons, and two of the General's brothers. These
young men were married, and several of them
were accompanied by their wives and children,
and distinguished only by their Christian
names; so that during the two days which I
spent in this truly patriarchal house, it was impossible for me to find out their degrees of re-
lationship. The company assembled either in
the parlor or saloon, especially the men, from
the hour of breakfast to that of bed-time; but
the conversation was always agreeable and
well supported. If you were desirous of di-
versifying the scene, there were some good
French and English authors at hand. An excellent breakfast at nine o'clock, a sumptuous
dinner at two, tea and punch in the afternoon,
and an elegant little supper divided the day
most happily for those whose stomachs were
never unprepared. It is worth observing that
on this occasion, where fifteen or twenty people
(four of whom were strangers to the family
and the country) were assembled together, and
by bad weather forced to stay often in doors,
not a syllable was said about play. How many

parties of trictrac, whist, and lotto would with us have been the consequence of such obstinate bad weather!'' (Chastellux's ''Travels.'')

The observations of the Chevalier de Chastellux sufficiently contradict the charge of the Greenwich preacher that Virginia ladies were ''unequal to any interesting or refined conversation.''

Colonel Byrd, with his inimitable drollery, furnishes us bits of description from which we get pictures of almost every rank of Virginia life in his time, 1732 (''Journey to the Mines''). He shows us the scolding overseer's wife; the widow expectant of a lover with ''an air becoming to a weed''; the spinster ''bewailing her virginity and expending her affections upon her dog''; the wife pushing on against all remonstrance through weather and mud to join her husband in the new settlement in Goochland; the family group at Tuckahoe listening to the ''Beggar's Opera'' read aloud; we get the tragical story ''of the young gentlewoman's marriage with her uncle's overseer,'' with the Colonel's reflection that ''had she run away with a gentleman or a pretty fellow there might have been some excuse for her, though he were of inferior fortune, but to stoop to a dirty ple-

beian without any kind of merit is the lowest
prostitution''; we see the elegant home of Colonel Spotswood at Germana, surrounded by its
garden and terraced walks, the tame deer coming into the house, smashing the pier glass,
knocking over the tea-table, and committing
havoc with the china, and giving Mrs. Spotswood the opportunity to show her calm and
beautiful temper; the gentlemen walking in the
garden discussing iron manufacture and politics; the ladies taking the visitor to see their
''small animals,'' their fowls; the rides about
the woods; the fine appetites and capital cheer.
It is a pleasant picture.

As we come down the century the prospect
simply widens; the gentry live upon their great
estates, working their tobacco, managing their
slaves and the affairs of the colony; breeding
their fine horses, and racing them in good old
English style; asserting and maintaining their
privileges; dispensing a lavish and lordly hospitality; visiting and receiving visits; marrying
and giving in marriage; their wives rolling
about in their coaches-and-four, dressed in
satins and brocades brought in their own ships
from London; their daughters in fine raiment,
often made by their own fair hands (''Journal

of a Young Lady of Virginia"), dancing, reading, and marrying; vying with their husbands and lovers in patriotism; sealing up their tea, and giving up all silk from England except for hats and bonnets (a charming touch); their sons going to William and Mary or across to Oxford or Cambridge, and growing up like their sires, gay, pleasure-loving, winning and losing garters on wagers, jealous of privilege, proud, assertive of their rights, ready to fight and stake all on a point of principle, and forming that society which was the virile soil from which sprang this nation.

Here is an "Inventory of Wedding Clothes" of one of the daughters of the Nelson House, at Yorktown:

A fashionable Lushing Sacque and Coat,
A rose white Satin Sacque and Coat,
A fine suit of Mechlin lace,
A fashionable Lushing gown,
A white Sattin Capuchin and bonnet,
A white Sattin quilted petticoat,
One piece of purple and white linen,
One piece of dark brown cotton,
One piece of fine corded dimity,
One piece of Cambrick, One piece ditto colored,
Six fine lawn handkerchiefs with striped borders,
Two fine sprigged lawn aprons,

Six pair Greshams, black Calamanca pumps,
Two pair green leather, two pair purple leather
    pumps,
One pair ditto white Sattin, one pair ditto pink,
One ditto white Sattin embroidered,
One dozen pair women's best woolen stockings,
Two pair ditto white silk,
One dozen women's best French gloves,
One ditto mitts,
One pound pins, one ditto short whites,
One pair tanned stays,
One pound of best Scotch thread sorted,
Six white silk laces, one set of combs,
A fashionable stomacher and knot,
Two Ivory stick fans,
A wax necklace and earrings,
A pink Sattin quilted petticoat,
Two fashionable gaus caps, one ditto blonde lace.

The time-stained record does not state who
was the fortunate lover of the little lady who
wanted the "fashionable lushing sacque and
coat," and other "fashionable" articles; but I
know she looked charming in her "white sattin
capuchin and bonnet," her "rose white sattin
sacque and coat," and her dainty "white sattin
embroidered pumps." What pretty feet she
must have had to have been so careful about
her "pumps,"—thirteen pair she ordered. I
wonder whose grandmother she was!

THE OLD SOUTH

No pen could do justice to the fair bride of the "white sattin capuchin and bonnet"; but here is a picture of a young gentleman of the period drawn by himself and furnished me by a descendant of the gentleman to whom the letters were addressed. The writer is Mr. Peter Randolph, of Chatsworth, and the letters are to his friend, Mr. Carr. They have never before been published, and are worth giving in full.

DEAR CARR:—Your attack upon the barrenness of entertainment which universally pervades James River, I acknowledge to be supported by the strictest justice, . . . Providence never formed a place in which dullness and melancholy held such extensive empire as on the once festive banks of James River. . . . You mention that you have heard I was paying my addresses to J. Randolph. Whoever informed you that I was actually laying siege to her too well defended castle did not obtain his information from a proper source. I confess I most sincerely love her; but I am so apprehensive of a frown from the terrific brows of her old mother that I am afraid to venture to Tuckahoe. There she is at present and there she will be for some time. However, even at the expense of a horse-whipping from the old beldame, I must shortly make a commencement, fame having so universally spread my intentions that I shall be accused of fickleness if I do not proceed. Something tho' more power-

ful than that would urge me to the attack, viz. :
a most serious and unalterable attachment. But
pray, my dear friend, where did you obtain your
information with respect to E. N. and what is the
purport of it? Who is your author? By heaven,
I still have a sincere regard for her; and tho' fettered
by love in another quarter cou'd I succeed with her,
rather than run the risk of losing either prize, I
wou'd make an attack upon her who seemed most
disposed to favour me. I think it wou'd make a
curious question in morals whether or no love can
be at the same time real and duplicate? It wou'd
seem curious to support the affirmative, but if I can
form any idea of the feelings of others by myself,
if I am not of a mould and composition entirely
different from the rest of my species, it may be supported with success. If I were to be this moment
executed I do not know which of these two girls I
love most; and yet I declare for each I have a most
violent fondness. With either of them I know I
cou'd be perfectly happy, and with either I shou'd
of course be content. When J. R. is present I think
the scale of affection preponderates in her favour.
When E. N. is with me, I feel a superior fondness
for her, and when both are absent, I cannot deter-
mine who can justly claim the superiority. Pray
write me by the next post every thing you have
heard relating to E. N. and you may depend on the
greatest secrecy: also, your author that I may be
able to judge what credit may be given to his report.
Remember me to all friends and as usual I am

Your Friend, PETER RANDOLPH.

157

This letter, though without date, must have been prior to the one following; for the writer has evidently decided to try J. R. and has even braved a frown from the terrific brows of the "old beldame," her mother. Here is the other:

July 28th, 1787.

DEAR CARR:—The requisitions of a friend are always to me most pleasing commands, which whilst they carry with them all the force of obedience of which the mandates of an Eastern despot can boast, nevertheless convey the most unfeigned satisfaction. They are, to be sure, marks of esteem and confidence which the man who makes them thinks can no where be so properly placed as in the person of whom he solicits the favour. I really tho' was somewhat surprised when I found your request of the nature it was. I did not suppose there was a man in the world to whom the history of my transactions could have afforded the smallest entertainment. ["Transactions" is good.] To be sure if originality has any right to attention many of my adventures may lay claim to it. But the originality was of so peculiar a nature that I supposed there were but few who could divine any satisfaction from hearing it. However, as I have found you of so extraordinary a mould as to wish the trifling satisfaction, as you have even particularly requested it, I shall conclude you are one of the few to whom the originality of P. R.'s original maneuvres are pleasing and interesting and shall therefore give you the whole history. I set out from Chatsworth on Monday, accompanied by old Abraham, on my way to Tuckahoe, resolved, if possible, to storm the citadel in which was contained Miss Judah's virtue and accomplishments. I first regulated my wardrobe as follows: I laid out for my first day's appearance; a thin and genteel riding coat and waistcoat, a pair of Nankeen breeches, white stockings and a beautiful pair of half boots. This you observe was for the first day's exhibition when mounted on the little roane I appeared at the terrestrial elysium Tuckahoe. The next thing on the docket was my red coat, in all its pristine effulgence glittering in the sun as if trimmed with gold. The black silk breeches which you, Champ, and myself got a pair of; a nice silk waistcoat and a pair of most elegant white silk stockings. For the next, a very elegant lead-coloured coat, a pair of Nankeen breeches, and very fine cotton stockings, with a most elegant dimmety waistcoat. This, sir, was the manner in which my extensive wardrobe was to be regulated. At the expiration of these three days, as I shou'd have sho'n all my cloaths I imagined they wou'd be nearly tired of me, I proposed taking my departure. But after having reached Richmond, some money which I expected to get there cou'd not be obtained. I thought it most prudent, therefore, to send old Abraham on and follow him in the morning. For you know nothing so soon signalizes a man as a fine gentleman, as being able to say to one servant, here, my boy, take this dollar for the trouble I have given you since my arrival, and to another this half dollar and so on. But to proceed with my story. When the morning arrived I found it as impossible to obtain money as I had done the night before. So I resolved to depend altogether on my own merit and go without. As I was going on in full tilt, I met Colonel Tom himself, who persuaded me much to stay and dine with him that day at Pennock's, and take the cool of the evening for it, as it was then very warm. I for some time hesitated, but considering from whom the request came I resolved to assent. I spent a very agreeable day at Pennock's, and the evening coming on apace I mounted my horse to go but had not proceeded far before I was stopped by the rain. In this dilemma nothing cou'd exceed my anxiety. I had sometimes an inclination to push thro' the violent storm, let the consequence be what it wou'd; for I was afraid lest old Abraham, who had gone up the night before carrying a huge portmanteau wou'd give me out and return. My prognostication proved too true. Early in the morning on which I intended to set out, who shou'd I see pacing into town but the old fellow with his portmanteau. Nothing cou'd now exceed my distress. I hated not to go, and still feared to set out for Tuckahoe. However, I changed my cloaths, dressed very genteelly, and resolved to set out unaccompanied by a servant. Doctr. Currie happened to be going up to visit Mrs. Randolph and we both pushed off together. After an agreeable ride we at length reached the house about 2 o'clock, just about the time when Miss J.'s beauty was in its meridian splendor. We found her doing the honours of the table with the most ineffable sweetness and grace. She rose as we entered to salute us. She rose! heavens with what angelic majesty tempered with all that sweetness and modesty of which human nature in its most perfect state is capable. If, Carr, you have never known the force of beauty. If you have been never warmed by the genial influence of love and are anxious not to experience its powerful effects until you have seen the sun of several years more, you may account yourself fortunate that you were not present at this interesting and commanding moment. The coldest anchorite who had not for 20 years before been agitated by the sudden impulse of any human passion, whose heart was formed of such insensible materials that his joy had never curdled at another's woe, who had not once in his whole life experienced the magic influence of a beautiful woman on the human soul, wou'd on this occasion have found that the ice of nature was converted into heat, and that he himself was re-animated into something more similar to the genius and disposition of a son of Adam. As she spoke to me a small border of red, occasioned by the blush of ingenuous modesty, tinged her lovely face, which opposed to the snowy whiteness of her skin formed an enchanting spectacle not much inferior to that which is exhibited in the eastern sky, just at the moment when aurora is about to dispense the beams of her effulgence to the whole animate world. For my part, I own I was transported with rapture, especially as I thought myself the cause of her making so lovely an appearance. What her blushes proceeded from I cannot tell, unless it was the eyes of the whole household fixing upon us two since every member of the family knew my attachment to her and conceived I had come with determination to pay my addresses to her. Be that as it may, I sat down to dinner but cou'd scarcely swallow a mouthful. My hand trembled, my heart palpitated and my eyes too well evinced my eternal commotion. After dinner we assembled in the hall where the sweet Judah favored us with a good deal of her incomparable musick. She played as if she had been inspired by some deity of musick, and tho' excelling in so peculiar a manner, seemed to do it with a modesty which appeared to indicate an opinion of her own deficiency which few so eminent as herself wou'd have thought they possessed. Thus my friend, have I endeavoured as circumstantially as possible to give you an account of my visit to the most perfect of her sex. In doing this I think I have said enough of her to enable you to form a proper idea of her worth. Shou'd you have been unfortunate enough not to have attained this knowledge, believe me when I tell you in plain words; She is beautiful, sensible, affable, polite, good-tempered, agreeable and to crown the whole, truly calculated both by her virtues and accomplishments to render any man happy.

Your friend, PETER S. RANDOLPH.

[This admirable summing up of his lady-love's virtues shows that the young coxcomb was at bottom a very sensible fellow.]

N.B.—If I can get the Nankeen for you I will, and

have it made by Bob who, I assure you, will make it better and cheaper than any Taylor down there. Get your measure and inclose it to me and the breeches shall be done as quick as possible.

With true wit he gives not a hint of the outcome of his expedition.

After the close of the Revolution there came a period in which the conditions were somewhat changed. The rights for which the colonies had contended had been recognized; independence had been secured; success, full and satisfying, had been achieved. Much military renown had been won. Meantime, the government of the States had been formed and established on a basis which satisfied the thoughtfulness and high-mindedness of the constructors. But all this was not without cost.

The great fortunes had melted away in the patriotic fervor of the owners. The men who made the war and won it paid for it. George Mason had found his wish gratified; he had got the liberty for which he had striven, and with it had got also the crust of bread with which he had promised to be contented. The wealthiest man in Virginia, Thomas Nelson, Jr., who had been the Revolutionary governor of Virginia, and the commander-in-chief of her forces, leading them in person, and at Yorktown pointing the guns at his own mansion, had pledged his entire private fortune for the pay of the troops, and had afterwards, in his seat as a Virginia representative, upon a motion to repudiate British claims, sworn that others might do as they pleased, but as for him, so help him God, he would pay his debts like an honest man. This he had done. When he died, on one of his outlying places, of exposure and overwork, it is tradition that his body was conveyed away in the night and carried to his home to avoid the danger of having it seized by rapacious creditors. His widow, formerly the wealthiest woman in Virginia, was left in her old age with but one piece of property, her children's mammy. Other fortunes had gone likewise.

The stern demands of war had welded the different elements into an extraordinarily homogeneous people. The sudden creation of a new government which was participated in by all and had done away with privilege, had given every one a personal interest in the State. At the same time the methods of life of those who had been the leaders had given the standard, and whether it was in the Tidewater or Piedmont, in the valley or beyond the mountain, land-holding in considerable quantity, and planter life in its carelessness and lavishness, became the style in vogue.

The new order found the Virginian established in his habits and exhibiting in his life a distinctive civilization with which he was entirely content and which he proposed to preserve and transmit to his children.

There was naturally the destruction of the equipoise which always succeeds war; the impairment of values, the change in the relation of things, which is the consequence of such a convulsion; the great fortunes went to pieces in the storm and left only the débris, to which the owners clung till they, too, were swept away by the currents. But if the Virginians came out of the war broken in fortune, they had gained an accession of spirit. What they had lost in wealth they had more than gained in pride. The fire of the seven years' struggle had tried their metal and proved its quality. The glory of the victory was in large part theirs. Their sons had behaved with gallantry on every field. A Virginian had become the personification of American valor and success. Victory seemed embodied in George Washington. The mighty men were yet in the prime of their intellectual vigor; they had sprung suddenly from subjects fighting for their rights, to peers owning no superiors, to law-makers knowing no laws but those which they framed. If they were proud they were likewise great. What they did was on a grand scale. To aid the country she had preserved; to establish the United States which without her could not have been, the great State changed her government, surrendered her incomparable position, and with a splendid generosity which was little appreciated and ill requited, ceded her vast transmontane possessions. She continued to maintain her prestige. In all public matters her sons continued to take the lead. President after president was chosen from among them. Her Marshall was selected to preside over the highest tribunal of the land as chief justice, and by the extraordinary powers which he displayed at once took place amongst the great judges of the world. She had already taken her position as the greatest colonizer of modern times. Kentucky beyond the mountains was really but her western district, settled by her sons, who had planted there Virginian homes and established in them the Virginian faith and customs.

But her sons had also gone elsewhere; South

166

and West they turned their faces, carrying their Virginian blood and social life, and planting wherever they settled a little Virginian colony which gave to that place something of the Virginia spirit.

A traveller sailing to Virginia, records that when two days from the coast, "the air was richly scented with the fragrance of the pine trees, wafted to them across the sea." In the same way, far beyond her borders was felt the Virginian influence sweetening and purifying the life of the people.

SOCIAL LIFE IN OLD VIRGINIA
BEFORE THE WAR

SOCIAL LIFE IN OLD VIRGINIA BEFORE THE WAR

LET me see if I can describe an old Virginia home recalled from a memory stamped with it when it was a virgin page. It may, perhaps, be idealized by the haze of time; but it will be as I now remember it.

The house was a plain "weather-board" building, one story and a half above the half-basement ground floor, set on a hill in a grove of primeval oaks and hickories filled in with ash, maples, and feathery-leafed locusts without number. It was built of timber cut by the "servants" (they were never termed slaves except in legal documents) out of the virgin forest, not long after the Revolution, when that branch of the family moved from Yorktown. It had quaint dormer windows, with small panes, poking out from its sloping upstairs rooms, and long porches to shelter its walls from the sun and allow house life in the open air.

A number of magnificent oaks and hickories (there had originally been a dozen of the former, and the place from them took its name, "Oakland,") under which Totapottamoi children may have played, spread their long arms about it, sheltering nearly a half-acre apiece; while in among them and all around were a few ash and maples, an evergreen or two, lilacs and syringas and roses, and locusts of every age and size, which in springtime filled the air with honeyed perfume, and lulled with the "murmur of innumerable bees."

There was an "office" in the yard; another house where the boys used to stay, and the right to sleep in which was as eagerly looked forward to and as highly prized as was by the youth of Rome the wearing of the *toga virilis*. There the guns were kept; there the dogs might sleep with their masters, under, or occasionally, in cold weather, even on, the beds; and there charming bits of gossip were retailed by the older young gentlemen, and delicious tales of early wickedness related, all the more delightful because they were veiled in chaste language phrased not merely to meet the doctrine, *maxima reverentia pueris debetur,* but to meet the higher truth that no gentleman would use foul language.

Off to one side was the orchard, in springtime a bower of pink and snow, and always making a pleasant spot in the landscape; beyond which peeped the ample barns and stables.

The fields that stretched around were poor, and in places red "galls" showed through, but the tillage was careful and systematic. At the best, it was a boast that a dish of blackberries could not be got on the place. The brown worm fences ran in lateral lines across, and the ditches were kept clean except for useful willows.

The furniture was old-timey and plain; mahogany and rosewood bedsteads and dressers black with age, and polished till they shone like mirrors, hung with draperies white as snow; straight-backed chairs generations old interspersed with common new ones; long sofas; old shining tables with slender, brass-tipped legs, straight or fluted, holding some fine old books, and in springtime a blue or flowered bowl or two with glorious roses; bookcases filled with brown-backed, much-read books. This was all.

The servants' houses, smoke-house, wash-house, and carpenter shop were set around the "back yard" with "mammy's house" a little nicer than the others; and farther off, upon and beyond the quarters hill, "the quarters"— whitewashed, substantial buildings, each for a family, with chicken-houses hard by, and with or without yards closed in by split palings, filled with fruit trees, which somehow bore cherries, peaches, and apples in a mysterious profusion even when the orchard failed.

The gardens (there were two: the vegetable garden and the flower garden) were separate. The former was the test of the mistress's power; for at the most critical times she took the best hands on the place to work it. The latter was the proof of her taste. It was a strange affair; pyrocanthus hedged it on the outside; honeysuckle ran riot over its palings, perfuming the air; yellow cowslips in well-regulated tufts edged some borders, while sweet peas, pinks, and violets spread out reck-lessly over others; jonquilles yellow as gold, and, once planted, blooming every spring as certainly as the trees budded or the birds nested, grew in thick bunches, and everywhere were tall lilies, white as angels' wings and stately as the maidens that walked among them; big snowball bushes blooming with snow, lilacs purple and white and sweet in the spring, and always with birds' nests in them with the bluest of eggs; and in places rosebushes, and tall holly-hock stems filled with rich rosettes of every hue and shade, made a delicious tangle. In the autumn rich dahlias and pungent-odored chrys-anthemums closed the season.

But the flower of all others was the rose. There were roses everywhere; clambering roses over the porches and windows, sending their fragrance into the rooms; roses beside the walks; roses around the yard and in the garden; roses of every hue and delicate refinement of perfume; rich yellow roses thick on their briery bushes, coming almost with the dandelions and buttercups, before any others dared face the April showers to learn if March had truly gone, sweet as if they had come from Paradise to be worn upon young maidens' bosoms, as they might well have done—who knows?—followed by the Giant of Battles on their stout stems, glorious enough to have been the worthy badge of victorious Lancastrian kings; white Yorks hardly less royal; cloth-of-golds; dainty teas; rich damasks; old sweet hundred-leafs sifting down their petals on the grass, and always filling with two the place where one had fallen. These and many more made the air fragrant, while the catbirds and mocking-birds fluttered and sang among them, and the robins foraged in the grass for their yellow-throated little ones waiting in the half-hidden nests.

Looking out over the fields was a scene not to be forgotten. Let me give it in the words of one who knew and loved Virginia well, and was her best interpreter—Dr. George W. Bagby. His "Old Virginia Gentleman" is perhaps the best sketch yet written in the South. To it I am doubtless indebted for much that I say in this paper. His description might do for a picture of Staunton Hill resting in delicious calm on its eminence above the Staunton River.

"A scene not of enchantment, though contrast often made it seem so, met the eye. Wide, very wide fields of waving grain, billowy seas of green or gold as the season chanced to be, over which the scudding shadows chased and played, gladdened the heart with wealth far spread. Upon lowlands level as the floor the plumed and tasselled corn stood tall and dense, rank behind rank in military alignment—a serried army lush and strong. The rich, dark soil of the gently swelling knolls [it was not always rich] could scarcely be seen under the broad lapping leaves of the mottled tobacco. The hills were carpeted with clover. Beneath the tree-clumps fat cattle chewed the cud, or peaceful sheep reposed, grateful for the shade. In the midst of this plenty, half hidden in foliage, over which the graceful shafts of the Lombard poplar towered, with its bounteous garden and its orchards heavy with fruit near at hand, peered the old mansion, white, or dusky red, or mellow gray by the storm and shine of years.

"Seen by the tired horseman halting at the woodland's edge, this picture, steeped in the intense quivering summer moonlight, filled the soul with unspeakable emotions of beauty, tenderness, peace, home.

"How calm could we rest
In that bosom of shade with the friends we love best!

"Sorrows and care were there—where do they not penetrate? But, oh! dear God, one day in those sweet tranquil homes outweighed a fevered lifetime in the gayest cities of the globe. Tell me nothing; I undervalue naught that man's heart delights in. I dearly love operas and great pageants; but I do know—as I know nothing else—that the first years of human life, and the last, yea, if it be possible, all the years, should be passed in the country. The towns may do for a day, a week, a month at most; but Nature, Mother Nature, pure and clean, is for all time; yes, for eternity itself.''

The life about the place was amazing. There were the busy children playing in troops, the boys mixed up with the little darkies as freely as any other young animals, and forming the associations which tempered slavery and made the relation one of friendship. There they were stooping down and jumping up; turning and twisting their heads close together, like chickens over an ''invisible repast,'' their active bodies always in motion, busy over their little matters with that ceaseless energy of boyhood which could move the world could it but be concentrated and conserved. They were all over the place; in the orchard robbing birds' nests, getting into wild excitement over catbirds, which they ruthlessly murdered because

178

they "called snakes"; in spring and summer fishing or "washing" in the creek, riding the plough-horses whenever they could, running the calves and colts, and being as mischievous as young mules.

There were the little girls in their great sun-bonnets, often sewed on to preserve the wonderful peach-blossom complexions, with their small female companions playing about the yard or garden, running with and wishing they were boys, and getting scoldings from mammy for being tomboys and tearing their aprons and dresses. There, in the shade, near her "house," was the mammy and her assistants, with her little charge in her arms, sleeping in her ample lap, or toddling about her, with broken, half-framed phrases, better understood than formed. There passed young negro girls, blue-habited, running about bearing messages; or older women moving at a statelier pace, doing with deliberation the little jobs which were their "work"; while about the office, or smoke-house, or dairy, or wood-pile there were always some movement and life. The recurrent hum on the air of spinning-wheels, like the drone of some great insect, sounded from the cabins where the turbaned spinners spun their fleecy rolls into yarn for the looms which were clacking from the loom-rooms making home-spun for the plantation.

From the back yard and quarters the laughter of women and the shrill, joyous voices of children came. Far off, in the fields, the white-shirted "ploughers" followed singly their slow teams in the fresh furrows, wagons rattled and ox-carts crawled along, or gangs of hands in lines performed their work in the corn or tobacco fields, loud shouts and peals of laughter, mellowed by the distance, floating up from time to time, telling that the heart was light and the toil not too heavy.

At special times there was special activity: at ice-getting time, at corn-thinning time, at fodder-pulling time, at threshing-wheat time, but above all at corn-shucking time, at hog-killing time, and at "harvest." Harvest was spoken of as a season. It was a festival. The severest toil of the year was a frolic. Every "hand" was eager for it. It was the test of the men's prowess and the women's skill; for it took a man to swing his cradle through the long June days and keep up with the bare-necked, knotted-armed leader as he strode and swung his cradle ringing through the heavy wheat.

180

So it demanded a strong back and nimble fingers to "keep up" and bind the sheaves. The young men looked forward to it as the young bucks looked to the war-path. How gay they appeared, moving in oblique lines around the "great parallelograms," sweeping down the yellow grain, and, as they neared the starting-point, chanting with mellow voices the harvest song "Cool Water"! How musical was the cadence as, taking time to get their wind, they whetted their ringing blades in unison! There was never any loneliness; it was movement and life without bustle; while somehow, in the midst of it all, the house seemed to sit enthroned in perpetual tranquillity, with outstretched wings under its spreading oaks, sheltering its children like a great gray dove.

Even at night there was stirring about: the ring of an axe, the infectious music of the banjos, the laughter of dancers, the festive noise and merriment of the cabin, the distant, mellowed shouts of 'coon or 'possum hunters, or the dirge-like chant of some serious and timid wayfarer passing along the paths over the hills or through the woods, and solacing his lonely walk with religious song.

Such was the outward scene. What was there

within? That which has been much misunderstood; that which was like the roses, wasteful beyond measure in its unheeded growth and blowing; but sweet beyond measure, too, and filling with its fragrance not only the region round about, but sending it out unstintedly on every breeze that wandered by.

There were the master and the mistress; the old master and old mistress, the young masters and young mistresses, and the children; besides some aunts and cousins, and the relations or friends who did not live there, but were only always on visits.

Properly, the mistress should be mentioned first, as she was the most important personage about the home, the presence which pervaded the mansion, the master willingly and proudly yielding her the active management of all household matters and simply carrying out her directions, confining his ownership within the curtilage exclusively to his old "secretary," which on her part was as sacred from her touch as her bonnet was from his. There were kept mysterious folded papers, and equally mysterious parcels, frequently brown with the stain of dust and age. Had the papers been the lost sibylline leaves instead of old receipts and bills, and the parcels contained diamonds instead of long-dried melon-seed or old flints, now out of date but once ready to serve a useful purpose, they could not have been more sacredly guarded by the mistress. The master generally had to hunt for a long period for any particular paper, whilst the mistress could in a half-hour have arranged everything in perfect order; but the chaos was regarded by her with veneration as real as that with which she regarded the mystery of the heavenly bodies. On the other hand, outside of this piece of furniture there was nothing which the master even pretended to know of. It was all in her keeping; whatever he wanted he called for and she produced with a certainty and promptness which appeared to him a perpetual miracle. Her system struck him as being the result of a wisdom as profound as that which fixed and held the firmament. He would not have dared to interfere, not because he was afraid, but because he recognized her superiority. It would no more have occurred to him to make a suggestion about the management of the house than about that of one of his neighbors, indeed not so readily; simply because he knew her and acknowledged her infallibility. She was, indeed, a surprising creature—often delicate and feeble in frame, and of a nervous organization so sensitive as to be a great sufferer; but her force and her character pervaded and directed everything, as unseen yet as unmistakably as the power of gravity controls the particles that constitute the earth.

It has been assumed by the outside world that our people lived a life of idleness and ease, a kind of "hammock-swung," "sherbet-sipping" existence, fanned by slaves, and, in their pride, served on bended knees. No conception could be further from the truth. The ease of the master of a big plantation was about that of the head of any great establishment where numbers of operatives are employed; and to the management of which are added the responsibilities of the care and complete mastership of the liberty of his operatives and their families. His work was generally sufficiently systematized to admit of enough personal independence to enable him to participate in the duties of hospitality; but any master who had a successfully conducted plantation was sure to have given it his personal supervision with an unremitting attention which would not have failed to secure success in any other calling. If this was true of the master, it was much more so of the mistress. The master might, by having a good overseer and reliable headmen, shift a portion of the burden from his shoulders; the mistress had no such means of relief. She was the necessary and invariable functionary; the keystone of the domestic economy which bound all the rest of the structure and gave it its strength and beauty. From early morn till morn again the most important and delicate concerns of the plantation were her charge and care. From superintending the setting of the turkeys to fighting a pestilence, there was nothing which was not her work. She was mistress, manager, doctor, nurse, counsellor, seamstress, teacher, housekeeper, slave, all at once. She was at the beck and call of every one, especially of her husband, to whom she was "guide, philosopher, and friend."

One of them, being told of a broken gate by her husband, said, "Well, my dear, if I could sew it with my needle and thread, I would mend it for you."

What she was only her husband knew, and even he stood before her in dumb, half-amazed admiration, as he might before the inscrutable vision of a superior being. What she really was, was known only to God. Her life was one long act of devotion—devotion to God, devotion to her husband, devotion to her children, devotion to her servants, to her friends, to the poor, to all humanity. Nothing happened within the range of her knowledge that her sympathy did not reach and her charity and wisdom did not ameliorate. She was the head and front of the church; an unmitred bishop *in partibus,* more effectual than the vestry or deacons, more earnest than the rector; she managed her family, regulated her servants, fed the poor, nursed the sick, consoled the bereaved. Who knew of the visits she paid to the cabins of her sick and suffering servants! often, at the dead of night, "slipping down" the last thing to see that her directions were carried out; with her own hands administering medicines or food; ever by her cheerlness inspiring new hope, by her strength giving courage, by her presence awaking faith; telling in her soft voice to dying ears the story of her suffering Saviour; soothing the troubled spirit, and lighting the path down into the valley of the dark shadow. What poor person was there, however inaccessible the cabin, that was sick or destitute and knew not her charity! who that was bereaved that had not her sympathy!

186

The training of her children was her work. She watched over them, inspired them, led them, governed them; her will impelled them; her word to them, as to her servants, was law. She reaped the reward. If she admired them, she was too wise to let them know it; but her sympathy and tenderness were theirs always and they worshipped her.

There was something in seeing the master and mistress obeyed by the plantation and looked up to by the neighborhood which inspired the children with a reverence akin to awe which is not known at this present time. It was not till the young people were grown that this reverence lost the awe and became based only upon affection and admiration. Then, for the first time, they dared to jest with her; then, for the first time, they took in that she was like them once, young and gay and pleasure-loving, with lovers suing for her; with coquetries and maidenly ways; and that she still took pleasure in the recollection—this gentle, classic, serious mother among her tall sons and radiant daughters. How she blushed as they laughed at her and teased her to tell of her conquests, her confusion making her look younger and prettier than they remembered her, and opening their eyes to the truth of what their father had told them so often, that not one of them was as beautiful as she.

She became timid and dependent as they grew up and she found them adorned with new fashions and ways which she did not know; she gave herself up to their guidance with a helpless kind of diffidence; was tremulous over her ignorance of the novel fashions which made them so beautiful; yet, when the exactions of her position came upon her, she took the lead, and, by her instinctive dignity, her self-possession, and her force, eclipsed them all as naturally as the full moon in heaven dims the stars.

As to the master himself it is hard to generalize. Yet there were indeed certain generic characteristics, whether he was quiet and severe, or jovial and easy. There was the foundation of a certain pride based on self-respect and consciousness of power. There were nearly always the firm mouth with its strong lines, the calm, placid, direct gaze, the quiet speech of one who is accustomed to command and have his command obeyed; there was a contemplative expression due to much communing alone, with

188

weighty responsibilities resting upon him; there was absolute self-confidence, and often a look caused by tenacity of opinion. There was not a doubtful line in the face nor a doubtful tone in the voice; his opinions were convictions; he was a partisan to the backbone; he was generally incapable of seeing more than one side. This prevented breadth, but gave force. He was proud, but never haughty except to dishonor. To that he was inexorable. He believed in God, he believed in his wife, he believed in his blood. He was chivalrous, he was generous, he was usually incapable of fear or meanness. To be a Virginia gentleman was the first duty; it embraced being a Christian and all the virtues. He lived as one; he left it as a heritage to his children. He was fully appreciative of both the honors and the responsibilities of his position. He believed in a democracy, but understood that the absence of a titled aristocracy had to be supplied by a class more virtuous than he believed them to be. This class was, of course, that to which he belonged. He purposed in his own person to prove that this was practicable. He established that it was. This and other responsibilities made him grave. He had inherited gravity from his father and grandfather before him. The latter had been a performer in the greatest work of modern times, with the shadow of the scaffold over him if he failed. The former had faced the weighty problems of the new government, with ever many unsolved questions to answer. He himself faced problems not less grave. The greatness of the past, the time when Virginia had been the mighty power of the New World, loomed ever above him. It increased his natural conservatism. He saw the change that was steadily creeping on. The conditions that had given his class their power and prestige had altered. The fields were worked down, and agriculture that had made his class rich no longer paid. The cloud was already gathering in the horizon; the shadow already was stretching towards him. He could foresee the danger that threatened Virginia. A peril ever sat beside his door. He was "holding the wolf by the ears." Outside influences hostile to his interest were being brought to bear. Any movement must work him injury. He sought the only refuge that appeared. He fell back behind the Constitution that his fathers had helped to establish, and became a strict constructionist for Virginia and his rights. These things made him grave. He reflected much. Out on the long verandas in the dusk of the summer nights, with his wide fields stretching away into the gloom, and "the woods" bounding the horizon, his thoughts dwelt upon serious things; he pondered causes and consequences; he resolved everything to prime principles. He communed with the Creator, and his first work, Nature.

He was a wonderful talker. He discoursed of philosophy, politics, and religion. He read much, generally on these subjects, and read only the best. His book-cases held the masters (in mellow Elzevirs and Lintots) who had been his father's friends, and with whom he associated and communed more intimately than with his neighbors. Horace, Virgil, Ovid, Shakespeare, Milton, Dryden, Goldsmith, "Mr. Pope," were his poets; Bacon, Burke, and Dr. Johnson were his philosophers. These "new fellows" that his sons raved over he held in so much contempt that his mere statement of their inferiority was to his mind an all-convincing argument.

Yet, if he was generally grave, he was at times, among his intimates and guests, jovial, even gay. On festive occasions no one surpassed him in cheeriness. When the house was full of guests he was the life of the company.

191

He led the prettiest girl out for the dance. At Christmas he took her under the mistletoe and paid her compliments which made her blush and courtesy with dimpling face and dancing eyes. But whatever was his mood, whatever his surroundings, he was always the exponent of that grave and knightly courtesy which under all conditions has become associated with the title "Virginia gentleman."

Whether or not the sons were, as young men, peculiarly admirable may be a question. They possessed the faults and the virtues of young men of their kind and condition. They were much given to self-indulgence; they were not broad in their limitations; they were apt to contemn what did not accord with their own established views (for their views were established before their mustaches); they were wasteful of time and energies beyond belief; they were addicted to the pursuit of pleasure, and blind to opportunities which were priceless. They exhibited the customary failings of their kind in a society of an aristocratic character. But they possessed in full measure the corresponding virtues. They were brave, they were generous, they were high-spirited. Indulgence in pleasure did not destroy them. It was the young French noblesse who affected to eschew exertion even to the point of having themselves borne on litters on their boar-hunts, who yet, with a hundred pounds of iron buckled on their frames, charged like furies at Fontenoy. So these same languid, philandering young gentlemen of Virginia at the crucial time suddenly appeared as the most dashing and indomitable soldiery of modern times. It was the Norfolk company known as the "Dandies" that was extirpated in a single day.

But, whatever may be thought of the sons, there can be no question as to the daughters. They were like the mother; made in her own image. They filled a peculiar place in the civilization; the key was set to them; they held by a universal consent the first place in the system, all social life revolving around them. So generally did the life shape itself about the young girl that it was almost as if a bit of the age of chivalry had been blown down the centuries and lodged in the old State. She instinctively adapted herself to it. In fact, she was made for it. She was gently bred: her people for generations (since they had come to Virginia) were gentlefolk. They were so well satisfied that they had been the same in the mother country that they had never taken the trouble to investigate it. She was the incontestable proof of their gentility. In right of her blood (the beautiful Saxon, tempered by the influences of the genial Southern clime), she was exquisite, fine, beautiful; a creature of peach-blossom and snow; languid, delicate, saucy; now imperious, now melting, always bewitching. She was not versed in the ways of the world, but she had no need to be; she was better than that; she was well bred. She had not to learn to be, because she was born a lady. Generations had given her that by heredity. But ignorance of the world did not make her provincial. Her instinct was an infallible guide. When a child she had in her sunbonnet and apron met the visitors at the front steps and entertained them in the parlor until her mother was ready. Thus she had grown up to the duties of hostess. Her manners were as perfectly formed as her mother's, with perhaps a shade more self-possession. Her beauty was a title which gave her a graciousness that befitted her. She never "came out," because she had never been in; and the line between girlhood and young-ladyhood was never known. She began to have beaux certainly before she reached the line; but it did her no harm: she would long walk herself "fancy free"; a protracted devotion was required of her lovers, and they began early. They were willing to serve long, for she was a prize worth winning. Her beauty, though it was often dazzling, was not her chief attraction; that was herself. It was that indefinable charm: the result of many attractions, in combination and in perfect harmony, which made her herself. She was delicate, she was dainty, she was sweet. She lived in an atmosphere created for her—the pure, clean, sweet atmosphere of her country home. She made its sunshine. She was a coquette, often an outrageous flirt. It did not imply heartlessness. It was said that the worst flirts made the most devoted wives. It was simply an instinct, an inheritance; it was in the life. Her heart was tender towards every living thing but her lovers; even to them it was soft in every way but one. Had they had a finger-ache she would have sympathized with them. But in the matter of love she was inexorable, remorseless. She played upon every chord of the heart. Perhaps it was because, when she gave up, the surrender was to be absolute. From the moment of marriage she was the worshipper. She was a strange being. Dressed in her mus-

lin and lawn, with her delicious, low, slow,
musical speech; accustomed to be waited on at
every turn, with servants to do her every bid-
ding, unhabituated often even to putting on her
dainty slippers or combing her soft hair, she
possessed a reserve force which was astounding.
She was accustomed to have her wishes obeyed
as commands. It did not make her imperious;
it simply gave her the habit of control. At marriage she was prepared to assume the duties of
mistress of her establishment, whether it were
great or small.

Thus, when the time came, the class at the
South which had been deemed the most supine
suddenly appeared as the most active and the
most indomitable. The courage which was displayed in battle was wonderful; but it was
nothing to what the Southern women exempli-
fied at home. There was perhaps not a doubtful woman within the limits of the Confederacy.
While their lovers and husbands fought in the
field, they performed the harder part of waiting
at home. With more than a soldier's courage
they bore more than a soldier's hardship. For
four long years they listened to the noise of the
guns, awaiting with blanched faces but undaunted hearts the news of battle after battle;

buried their beloved dead with tears, and still amid their tears encouraged the survivors to fight on. It was a force which has not been duly estimated. It was in the blood.

She was, indeed, a strange creature, that delicate, dainty, mischievous, tender, God-fearing, inexplicable Southern girl. With her fine grain, her silken hair, her satiny skin, her musical speech; pleasure-loving, saucy, bewitching—deep down lay the bed-rock foundation of innate virtue, piety, and womanliness, on which were planted all to which human nature can hope, and all to which it can aspire. Words fail to convey an idea of what she was; as well try to describe the beauty of the rose or the perfume of the violet. To appreciate her one must have seen her, have known her, have adored her.

There are certain characters without mention of which no description of the social life of old Virginia or of the South would be complete—the old mammies and family servants about the house. These were important functionaries. The mammy was the zealous, faithful, and efficient assistant of the mistress in all that pertained to the training of the children. Her authority was recognized in all that related to them directly or indirectly, second only to that of the mistress and master. She regulated them, disciplined them, having authority indeed in cases to administer correction. Her *régime* extended frequently through two generations, occasionally through three. From their infancy she was the careful and faithful nurse, the affection between her and the children she nursed being often more marked that that between her and her own children. She may have been harsh to the latter; she was never anything but tender with the others. Her authority was, in a measure, recognized through life, for her devotion was unquestionable. The young masters and mistresses were her "children" long after they had children of their own. They embraced her, when they parted from her or met with her again after separation, with the same affection as when in childhood she "led them smiling into sleep." She was worthy of the affection. At all times she was their faithful ally, shielding them, excusing them, petting them, aiding them, yet holding them up to a certain high accountability. Her influence was always for good. She received, as she gave, an unqualified affection; if she was a slave, she at least was not a servant, but was an honored member of the

"She was never anything but tender with the others."

family, universally beloved, universally cared for—"the Mammy."

Next to her were the butler and the carriage-driver. These were the aristocrats of the family, who trained the children in good manners and other exercises; and uncompromising aristocrats they were. The butler was apt to be severe, and was feared; the driver was genial and kindly, and was adored. I recall a butler, "Uncle Tom," an austere gentleman, who was the terror of the juniors of the connection. One of the children, after watching him furtively as he moved about with grand air, when he had left the room and his footsteps had died away, crept over and asked her grandmother, his mistress, in an awed whisper, "Grandma, are you 'fraid of Unc' Tom?" Perhaps even grandma stood a little in awe of him. The driver was the ally of the boys, and consequently had an ally in their mother, the mistress. As the head of the stable, he was an important personage in their eyes. This comradeship was never forgot; it lasted through life; the years might grow on him, but he was left in command even when he was too feeble to hold the horses; and to the end he was always "the Driver of Mistress's carriage."

Other servants there were with special places and privileges—gardeners and "boys about the house," comrades of the boys; and "own maids" of the ladies, for each girl had her "own maid"—they all formed one great family in the social structure now passed away, a structure incredible by those who knew it not, and now, under new conditions, almost incredible by those who knew it best.

The social life formed of these elements in combination was one of singular sweetness and freedom from vice. If it was not filled with excitement, it was replete with happiness and content. It is asserted that it was narrow. Perhaps it was. It was so sweet, so charming, that it is little wonder if it asked nothing more than to be let alone.

They were a careless and pleasure-loving people; but, as in most rural communities, their festivities were free from dissipation. There was sometimes too great an indulgence on the part of young men in the State drink—the julep; but whether it was that it killed early or that it was usually abandoned as the responsibilities of life increased, an elderly man of dissipated habits was almost unknown. They were fond of sport, and excelled in it, being generally fine shots and skilled hunters. Love of horses was a race characteristic, and fine horsemanship was a thing little considered only because it was universal.

The life was gay. In addition to the perpetual round of ordinary entertainment, there was always on hand or in prospect some more formal festivity—a club meeting; a fox-hunt; a party; a tournament; a wedding. Little excuse was needed to bring them together where every one was social, and where the great honor was to be the host. Scientific horse-racing was confined to the regular race-tracks, where the races were not little dashes, but four-mile heats which tested speed and bottom alike. But good blood was common, and a ride even with a girl in an afternoon generally meant a dash along the level through the woods, where, truth to tell, she was very apt to win. Occasionally there was even a dash from the church. The high-swung carriages, having received their precious loads of lily-fingered, pink-faced, laughing girls, with teeth like pearls and eyes like stars, helped in by young men who would have thrown not only their cloaks but their hearts into the mud to keep those dainty feet from being soiled, would go ahead; and then, the restive saddle-horses being untied from the swinging limbs, the young gallants would mount, and, by an instinctive common impulse, starting all together, would make a dash to the first hill, on top of which the dust still lingered, a nimbus thrown from the wheels that rolled their goddesses.

The chief sport, however, was fox-hunting. It was, in season, almost universal. Who that lived in Old Virginia does not remember the fox-hunts—the eager chase after ''grays'' or ''old reds''! The grays furnished more fun, the reds more excitement. The grays did not run so far, but usually kept near home, going in a circuit of six or eight miles. ''An old red,'' generally so called irrespective of age, as a tribute or respect for his prowess, was apt to lead the dogs all day, and might wind up by losing them as evening fell, after taking them in a dead stretch for thirty miles. The capture of a gray was what men boasted of; a chase after ''an old red'' was what they ''yarned'' about. Some old reds became historical characters, and were as well known and as much discussed in the counties they inhabited as the leaders of the bar or the crack speakers of the circuit. The wiles and guiles of each veteran were the pride of his neighbors and hunters. Many of them had names. Gentlemen discussed them at their club dinners; lawyers told stories about them in the "Lawyers' Rooms" at the court-houses; young men, while they waited for the preacher to get well into the service before going into church, bragged about them in the churchyards on Sundays. There was one such that I remember; he was known as "Nat Turner," after the notorious negro of that name, who, after inciting the revolt in South-ampton County, in the year 1832, known as "Nat Turner's Rebellion," in which some fifty persons were massacred, remained out in hiding for weeks after all his followers were taken before he was captured.

Great frolics these old red hunts were; for there were the prettiest girls in the world in the country houses around, and each young fellow was sure to have in his heart some brown-eyed or blue-eyed maiden to whom he had promised the brush, and to whom, with feigned indiffer-ence but with mantling cheek and beating heart, he would carry it if, as he counted on doing, he should win it. Sometimes the girls came over themselves and rode, or more likely were already there visiting, and the beaux followed them, and got up the hunt in their honor.

Even the boys had their sweethearts, and rode for them on the colts or mules: not the small girls of their own age (no, sir, no "little girls" for them)—their sweethearts were grown young ladies, with smiling eyes and silken hair and graceful mien, whom their grown cousins courted, and whom they with their boys' hearts worshipped. Often a half-dozen were in love with one—always the prettiest one—and, with the generous democratic spirit of boys in whom the selfish instinct has not awakened, agreed among themselves that they would all ride for her, and that which ever of them got the brush should present it on behalf of all.

What a sight it was! The appearance of the hunters on the far hill, in the evening, with their packs surrounding them! Who does not recall the excitement at the house; the arrival in the yard, with horns blowing, hounds baying, horses prancing, and girls laughing; the picture of the girls on the front portico with their arms around each other's dainty waists—the slender, pretty figures, the bright faces, the sparkling eyes, the gay laughter and musical voices as they challenged the riders with coquettish merriment, demanding to blow the horns themselves or to ride some specially handsome horse next morning! The way, the challenge being accepted, they tripped down the steps to get the horn, some shrinking from the bounding dogs with little subdued screams, one or two with stouter hearts, fixed upon higher game, bravely ignoring them and leaving their management to their masters, who at their approach sprang to the ground to meet them hat in hand and the telltale blood mounting to their sunburned faces, handsome with the beauty of youth!

I am painfully aware of the inadequacy of my picture. But who could do justice to the truth!

It was owing to all these and some other characteristics that the life was what it was. It was on a charming key. It possessed an ampleness and generosity which were not splendid because they were refined.

Hospitality had become a recognized race characteristic, and was practised as a matter of course. It was universal; it was spontaneous. It was one of the distinguishing features of the civilization; as much a part of the social life as any other of the domestic relations. Its generosity secured it a distinctive title. The exactions it entailed were engrossing. Its exercises occupied much of the time, and exhausted much of the means. The constant intercourse of the neighborhood, with its perpetual round of dinners, teas, and entertainments, was supplemented by visits of friends and relatives from other sections, who came, with their families, their equipages, and personal servants, to spend a month or two, or as long a time as they pleased. A dinner invitation was not so designated. It was with more exactitude, termed ''spending the day.'' On Sundays every one invited every one else from church, and there would be long lines of carriages passing in at the open gates.

It is a mystery how the house ever held the visitors. Only the mistress knew. Her resources were enormous. The rooms, with their low ceilings, were wide, and had a holding capacity which was simply astounding. The walls seemed to be made of india-rubber, so great was their stretching power. No one who came, whether friend or stranger, was ever turned away. If the beds were full—as when were they not!—pallets were put down on the floor in the parlor or the garret for the younger members of the family, sometimes even the passages being utilized. Often children spent half their lives on pallets "made up" on the floors. Frequently at Christmas the master and mistress were compelled to resort to the same refuge, their pallet being placed in the garret.

It was this intercourse, following the intermarriage and class feeling of the old families, which made Virginians clannish and caused a single distinguishable common strain of blood, however distant, to be counted as kinship.

Perhaps this universal entertainment might not now be considered elegant; perhaps.

It was based upon a sentiment as pure as can animate the human mind. It was easy, generous, and refined. The manners of the entertainers and entertained were gentle, cordial, simple, with, to strangers, a slight trace of stateliness.

The conversation was surprising; it was of the crops, the roads, politics, mutual friends, including the entire field of neighborhood matters, related not as gossip, but as affairs of common interest, which every one knew or was expected and entitled to know.

The fashions came in, of course, among the ladies, embracing particularly "patterns."

Politics took the place of honor among the

gentlemen, their range embracing not only State and national politics, but British as well, as to which they possessed astonishing knowledge, interest in English matters having been handed down from father to son as a class test. "My father's" opinion was quoted as a conclusive authority on this and all points, and in matters of great importance historically "my grandfather, sir," was cited. The peculiarity of the whole was that it possessed a literary flavor of a high order; for, as has been said, the classics, Latin and English, with a fair sprinkling of good old French authors, were in the bookcases, and were there not for show, but for companionship. There was nothing for show in that life; it was all genuine, real, true.

The great fête of the people was Christmas. Spring had its special delights: horseback rides through the budding woods, with the birds singing; fishing parties down on the little rivers, with out-of-doors lunches and love-making; parties of various kinds from house to house. Summer had its pleasures: handsome dinners, and teas with moonlight strolls and rides to follow; visits to or from relations, or even to the White Sulphur Springs, called simply "the White." The Fall had its pleasures. But all times and seasons paled and dimmed before the festive joys of Christmas. It had been handed down for generations; it belonged to the race. It had come over with their fore-fathers. It had a peculiar significance. It was a title. Religion had given it its benediction. It was the time to "Shout the glad tidings." It was The Holidays. There were other holi-days for the slaves, both of the school-room and the plantation, such as Easter and Whit-Mon-day; but Christmas was distinctively "The Holi-days." Then the boys came home from school or college with their friends; the members of the family who had moved away returned; pretty cousins came for the festivities; the neigh-borhood grew merry; the negroes were all to have holiday, the house-servants taking turn and turn about, and the plantation made ready for Christmas cheer. It was by all the younger population looked back to half the year, looked forward to the other half. Time was measured by it; it was either so long "since Christmas," or so long "before Christmas." The affairs of the plantation were set in order against it. The corn was got in; the hogs were killed; the lard "tried"; sausage-meat made; mince-meat pre-pared; the turkeys fattened, with "the old big gobbler'' specially devoted to the ''Christmas dinner''; the servants' new shoes and winter clothes stored away ready for distribution; and the plantation began to be ready to prepare for Christmas.

In the first place, there was generally a cold spell which froze up everything and enabled the ice-houses to be filled. [The seasons, like a good many other things, appear to have changed since the war.] This spell was the harbinger; and great fun it was at the ice-pond, where the big rafts of ice were floated along, with the boys on them. The rusty skates with their curled runners and stiff straps were got out, and maybe tried for a day. Then the stir began. The wagons all were put to hauling wood—hickory; nothing but hickory now; other wood might do for other times, but at Christmas only hickory was used; and the wood-pile was heaped high with logs; while to the ordinary wood-cutters ''for the house'' were added three, four, a half-dozen more, whose shining axes rang around the wood-pile all day long. With what a vim they cut, and how telling was that ''Ha'nh!'' as they drove the ringing axes into the hard wood, sending the big white chips flying! It was always the envy of the boys, that simultaneous, ostentatious expulsion of the breath, and they used vainly to try to imitate it.

In the midst of it came the wagon or the ox-cart from "the depot," with the big white boxes of Christmas things, the black driver feigning hypocritical indifference as he drove through the choppers to the storeroom. Then came the rush of all the wood-cutters to help him unload; the jokes among themselves, as they pretended to strain in lifting, of what "master" or "mistis" was going to give them out of those boxes, uttered just loud enough to reach their master's or mistress's ears where they stood looking on, while the driver took due advantage of his temporary prestige to give many pompous cautions and directions.

The getting the evergreens and mistletoe was the sign that Christmas had come, was really here. There were the parlor and hall and dining-room, and, above all, the old church, to be "dressed." The last was a neighborhood work; all united in it, and it was one of the events of the year. Young men rode thirty and forty miles to "help" dress that church. They did not go home again till after Christmas. The return from the church was the beginning of the festivities.

Then by "Christmas Eve's eve" the wood

was all cut and stacked high in the wood-house and on and under the back porticos, so as to be handy, and secure from the snow which was almost certain to come. Then came the snow. It seems that Christmas was almost sure to bring it in old times; at least it is closely associated with it. The excitement increased; the boxes were unpacked, some of them openly, to the general delight, others with a mysterious secrecy which stimulated the curiosity to its highest point and added to the charm of the occasion. The kitchen filled up with assistants famed for special skill in particular branches of the cook's art, who bustled about with glistening faces and shining teeth, proud of their elevation and eager to add to the general cheer.

It was now Christmas Eve. From time to time the "hired out" servants came home from Richmond or other places where they had been hired or had hired out themselves, their terms having been by common custom framed, with due regard to their rights to the holiday, to expire in time for them to spend the Christmas at home.[1] There was much hilarity over their arrival, and they were welcomed like members of the family as, with their new winter clothes

[1] The hiring contracts ran from New Year to Christmas.

212

donned a little ahead of time, they came to pay their "bespec's to master and mistis."

Then the vehicles went off to the distant station for the visitors—for the visitors and the boys. Oh, the excitement of that! the drag of the long hours at first, and then the eager expectancy as the time approached for their return; the "making up" of the fires in the visitors' rooms (of the big fires; there had been fires there all day "to air" them, but now they must be made up afresh); the hurrying backwards and forwards of the servants; the feverish impatience of every one, especially of the children, who are sure the train is late or that something has happened, and who run and "look up towards the big gate" every five minutes, notwithstanding the mammy's oft-repeated caution that a "watch' pot never b'iles." There was an exception to the excitement: the mistress, calm, deliberate, unperturbed, moved about with her usual composure, her watchful eyes seeing that everything was "ready" (her orders had been given and her arrangements made days before, such was her system). The girls, having finished dressing the parlor and hall, had disappeared. Satisfied at last with their work, after innumerable final touches, every one of which was an undeniable improvement to that which already appeared perfect, they had suddenly vanished—vanished as completely as a dream—to appear again later on at the parlor door, radiant visions of loveliness, or, maybe, if certain unlooked-for visitors unexpectedly arrived, to meet accidentally in the less embarrassing and safer precincts of the dimly lighted passages. When they appeared, what a transformation had taken place! If they were bewitching before, now they were entrancing. The gay, laughing, saucy creature who had been dressing the parlors and hanging the mistletoe with many jests and parries of the half-veiled references was now a demure or stately maiden in all the dignity of a new gown and with all the graciousness of a young countess.

But this is after the carriages return. They have not yet come. They are late—they are always late—and it is dark before they come; the glow of the fires and candles shines out through the windows on the snow, often blackened by the shadows of little figures whose noses are pressed to the panes, which grow blurred with their warm breath. Meantime the carriages, piled up outside and in, are slowly

"At last the 'big gate' is reached."

making their way homeward through the frozen roads, followed by the creaking wagon filled with trunks, on which are perched several small muffled figures, whose places in the carriages are taken by unexpected guests. The drivers still keep up a running fire with their young masters, though they have long since been pumped dry by "them boys" as to every conceivable matter connected with "home," in return for which they receive information as to school and college pranks. At last the "big gate" is reached; a half-frozen figure rolls out and runs to open it, flapping his arms in the darkness like some strange, uncanny bird; they pass through; the gleam of a light shines away off on a far hill. The shout goes up, "There she is; I see her!" The light is lost, but a little later appears again. It is the light in the mother's chamber, the curtains of the windows of which have been left up intentionally, that the welcoming gleam may be seen afar off by her boys on the first hill—a blessed beacon shining from home and her mother's heart.

Across the white fields the dark vehicles move, then toil up the house hill, filled with their eager occupants, who can scarce restrain themselves; approach the house, by this time glowing with lighted windows, and enter the yard just as the doors open and a swarm rushes out with joyful cries of "Here they are!" "Yes, here we are!" comes in cheery answer, and one after another they roll or step out, according to age and dignity, and run up the steps, stamping their feet, the boys to be taken fast into motherly arms, and the visitors to be given warm handclasps and cordial welcomes.

Later on the children were got to bed, scarce able to keep in their pallets for excitement; the stockings were all hung up over the big fireplace; and the grown people grew gay in the crowded parlors. Mark you, there was no splendor, nor show, nor style, as it would be understood now. Had there been, it could not have been so charming. There were only profusion and sincerity, heartiness and gayety, fun and merriment, cordiality and cheer, and withal genuineness and refinement.

Next morning before light the stir began. White-clad little figures stole about in the gloom, with bulging stockings clasped to their bosoms, opening doors, shouting "Christmas gift!" into dark rooms at sleeping elders, and then scurrying away like so many white mice, squeaking with delight, to rake open the embers and inspect their treasures. At prayers, "Shout the glad tidings" was sung by fresh young voices with due fervor.

How gay the scene was at breakfast! What pranks had been performed in the name of Santa Claus! Every foible had been played on. What lovely telltale blushes and glances and laughter greeted the confessions! The larger part of the day was spent in going to and coming from the beautifully dressed church, where the service was read, and the anthems and hymns were sung by everybody, for every one was happy.

But, as in the beginning of things, "the evening and the morning were the first day." Dinner was the great event. It was the test of the mistress and the cook, or, rather, the cooks; for the kitchen now was full of them. It is impossible to describe it. The old mahogany table, stretched diagonally across the dining-room, groaned; the big gobbler filled the place of honor; a great round of beef held the second place; an old ham, with every other dish that ingenuity, backed by long experience, could devise, was at the side, and the shining sideboard, gleaming with glass, scarcely held the dessert. The butler and his assistants were supernat-

urally serious and slow, which bespoke plainly
too frequent a recourse to the apple-toddy bowl;
but, under stimulus of the mistress's eye, they
got through all right, and their slight un-
steadiness was overlooked.

It was then that the fun began.

After dinner there were apple-toddy and egg-
nogg, as there had been before.

There were games and dances—country
dances, the lancers and quadrilles. The top of
the old piano was lifted up, and the infectious
dancing-tunes rolled out under the flying fingers.
There was some demur on the part of the elder
ladies, who were not quite sure that it was right;
but it was overruled by the gentlemen, and the
master in his frock coat and high collar started
the ball by catching the prettiest girl by the
hand and leading her to the head of the room
right under the noses of half a dozen bashful
lovers, calling to them meantime to "get their
sweethearts and come along." Round dancing
was not yet introduced. It was regarded as an
innovation, if nothing worse. It was held generally as highly improper, by some as "disgust-
ing." As to the german, why, had it been
known, the very name would have been sufficient
to damn it. Nothing foreign in that civilization!
There was fun enough in the old-fashioned

country dances, and the "Virginia reel" at the close; whoever could not be satisfied with that was hard to please.

There were the negro parties, where the ladies and gentlemen went to look on, the suppers having been superintended by the mistresses, and the tables being decorated by their own white hands. There was almost sure to be a negro wedding during the holidays. The ceremony might be performed in the dining-room or in the hall by the master, or in a quarter by a colored preacher; but it was a gay occasion, and the dusky bride's trousseau had been arranged by her young mistress, and the family was on hand to get fun out of the entertainment.

Other weddings there were, too, sometimes following these Christmas gayeties, and sometimes occurring "just so," because the girls were the loveliest in the world, and the men were lovers almost from their boyhood. How beautiful our mothers must have been in their youth to have been so beautiful in their age!

There were no long journeys for the young married folk in those times; the traveling was usually done before marriage. When a wedding took place, however, the entire neighborhood entertained the young couple.

Truly it was a charming life. There was a

vast waste; but it was not loss. Every one had food, every one had raiment, every one had peace. There was not wealth in the base sense in which we know it and strive for it and trample down others for it now. But there was wealth in a good old sense in which the litany of our fathers used it. There was weal. There was the best of all wealth; there was content, and ''a quiet mind is richer than a crown.''

We have gained something by the change. The South under her new conditions will grow rich, will wax fat; nevertheless we have lost much. How much only those who knew it can estimate; to them it was inestimable.

That the social life of the Old South had its faults I am far from denying. What civilization has not? But its virtues far outweighed them; its graces were never equalled. For all its faults, it was, I believe, the purest, sweetest life ever lived. It has been claimed that it was non-productive, that it fostered sterility. Only ignorance or folly could make the assertion. It largely contributed to produce this nation; it led its armies and its navies; it established this government so firmly that not even it could overthrow it; it opened up the great West; it added Louisiana and Texas, and more than

220

trebled our territory; it Christianized the negro race in a little over two centuries, impressed upon it regard for order, and gave it the only civilization it has ever possessed since the dawn of history. It has maintained the supremacy of the Caucasian race, upon which all civilization seems now to depend. It produced a people whose heroic fight against the forces of the world has enriched the annals of the human race —a people whose fortitude in defeat has been even more splendid than their valor in war. It made men noble, gentle, and brave, and women tender and pure and true. It may have fallen short in material development in its narrower sense, but it abounded in spiritual development; it made the domestic virtues as common as light and air, and filled homes with purity and peace.

It has passed from the earth, but it has left its benignant influence behind it to sweeten and sustain its children. The ivory palaces have been destroyed, but myrrh, aloes, and cassia still breathe amid their dismantled ruins.

TWO OLD COLONIAL PLACES

TWO OLD COLONIAL PLACES

I

OLD YORKTOWN

ONE hundred years ago, the eyes of a few colonies along the Atlantic seaboard were turned anxiously toward "Little York," a small town in Virginia, situated on the curve of York River, in Indian days the great "Pamunkee," just above where its white current mingles with the green waters of Chesapeake Bay. There was being fought the death struggle between Great Britain and her revolutionary colonies, —between the Old and the New.

Affairs had assumed a gloomy aspect. The army of the South had been defeated and driven back into Virginia, barely escaping annihilation by forced marches, and by the successful passage of the deep rivers which intersect the country through which it retreated; Virginia, the backbone of the Revolution, had been swept by two invasions; and Cornwallis with his victorious army was marching triumphantly through her borders, trying by every means he could devise to bring his only opponent, a young French officer, to an engagement. Had "the boy," Lafayette, proved as reckless as the British commander believed him, the end would have come before De Grasse with his fleet anchored in the Chesapeake. He was, however, no boy in the art of war, and at length Cornwallis, wearied of trying to catch him, retired to York, and intrenching himself, awaited reenforcements from the North. Just at this time, Providence directed the French admiral to the Virginia coast, and the American commander-in-chief, finding himself suddenly possessed of a force such as he had never hoped for in his wildest dreams, and knowing that he could count on the new re-enforcements for only a few weeks, determined to put his fate to the touch, and win if possible by a *coup de main*. With this end in view, he withdrew from New York, and came down to Jersey as if to get near his ovens, a move which misled the British commander, who knew that a good meal was a sufficient inducement to carry the hungry American troops farther than that, and did not suspect the ulterior object until he learned that Washington was well on his way to Virginia. In the last days of September, the colonial general arrived before York and threw the die. Before the end of three weeks, the British troops marched out with cased colors, prisoners of war. The details of the surrender included an act of poetic retribution. When General Lincoln had, not long before, surrendered at Charleston to Cornwallis, the British marquis appointed an inferior officer to receive his sword; this affront General Washington now avenged by appointing General Lincoln to receive Cornwallis's sword.

When the British prime minister received the intelligence of the surrender, he threw up his hands, exclaiming, "My God! it is all over!" And it was all over—America was free.

A hundred years have passed by since that time, and with natural pride the people of these United States are preparing to celebrate the centennial anniversary of the great event which secured their independence. Once more the little sleepy Virginia town, which has for a century lain as if under a spell, awakes with a start to find itself the centre of interest.

Had the siege of Yorktown taken place a dozen centuries ago, the assailants, instead of hammering the fortifications down as fast as they were repaired, might have been forced to wait until the grim ally, starvation, compelled the besieged to capitulate. Even at this day the place gives evidence of its advantages as a fortified camp. High ramparts and deep fosses, which might have satisfied a Roman consul, surround it on three sides, and on the fourth is a precipitous bluff above the deep, wide York which could be defended by a handful. These fortifications, however, have not come down from the Revolution; they bear witness to a later strife. Magruder began them in those early days of 1861, when each side thought the Civil War sport for a summer holiday; and later on, when the magnitude of the struggle was understood, McClellan strengthened them. Together with the few antique brick buildings with massive walls and peaked roofs, which have survived the assaults of three successive wars, and of that more insidious destroyer, Time, they give the place the impressiveness of an old walled town. All new ways and things seem to have been held at bay.

The town is about one hundred and eighty-five years old. It looks much older, but repeated wars have an aging effect.

Its founder was Thomas Nelson, a young settler from Penrith, on the border of Scotland, who was for that reason called "Scotch Tom." His father was a man of substance and position in Cumberland and was a warden of the church in Penrith. The warden's son Thomas looking to the New World to enlarge his fortune, after making one or two trips across, finally settled at the mouth of York River. Here he married Margaret Reid, and soon became one of the wealthiest men in the colony. His dwelling, known as the "Nelson House," still stands, with its lofty chimneys and solid walls—towering among the surrounding buildings; an enduring pre-eminence which would probably have gratified the pride which tradition says moved him to have the corner-stone passed through the hands of his infant heir. The massive door and small windows, with the solid shutters, look as if the house had been constructed more with a view to defence than to architectural grace. Within, everything is antique; modern paint has recently, with doubtful success, if not propriety, attempted to freshen up the old English wainscoting; but the old-time air of the place cannot be banished. Memory grows busy as she walks through the lofty rooms and recalls the scenes they have witnessed. Here, in "ye olden tyme," dwelt a race which grew to wealth and power noted even in that age, when the mere lapse of years, opening up the broad, wild lands to the westward, and multiplying the slaves, doubled and quadrupled their possessions without care or thought of the owners. Here, in this home of the Nelsons, have been held receptions at which have gathered Grymeses, Diggeses Custises, Carys, Blands, Lees, Carters, Randolphs, Burwells, Pages, Byrds, Spottswoods, Harrisons, and all the gay gentry of the Old Dominion. Up the circular stone steps, where now the dust of the street lies thick, blushing, laughing girls have tripped, followed by stately mammas, over whose precious heads the old-time "canopies" were held by careful young lovers, or lordly squires whose names were to become as imperishable as the great Declaration which they subscribed. Coming down to a later period, a more historical interest attaches itself to the mansion. George Mason and Washington and Jefferson have slept here; Cornwallis established his headquarters here during the last

days of the great siege, when his first headquarters, Secretary Nelson's house, had been
shelled to pieces. Even here the guns aimed
by the master of the mansion, then Governor of
Virginia and commander-in-chief of her forces,
reached him as the splintered rafters and the
solid shot stuck in the wall testify. Lafayette,
no longer the boyish adventurer with a mind
wild with romantic dreams of the Cid, and
chased like a fugitive by his sovereign, but the
honored and revered guest of a mighty nation,
returning in his old age to witness the greatness
of the New World toward which his valor had
so much contributed, slept here and added another to the many associations which already
surrounded the mansion.

Thomas Nelson, having built his house, died
and was buried in the churchyard of the old
church. His handsome tomb is one of the two
antique monuments which, in spite of war and
weather, still remain notable relics of old York.
It stands in the uninclosed common near the old
church on the bluff, not a stone's throw from
the centre of the town. On the four sides,
cherubs' faces, elaborately carved, look forth
from clouds. Once, a crown was being placed
on the head of one; another, trumpet in mouth,

was proclaiming "All glory to God," but the ascription under the wear and tear of time has disappeared. The weather and the vandal have marred and wasted the carving; but enough yet remains to show that on it some excellent sculptor used his utmost skill. The coat of arms on the top shows the *fleur de lis* as his crest, while the inscription and heraldic insignia declare the founder of Yorktown to have been a "gentleman." At his feet, beneath a less imposing tomb, lies Scotch Tom's eldest son, William Nelson, called "President" Nelson from his having been president of the King's Council, and, as such, during an interregnum, governor of the colony. At his feet, in turn, sleeps, in an unmarked grave, the president's eldest son, General Thomas Nelson, the most illustrious of the race, the mover in the great Virginia Convention of 1776 of the resolution first instructing her delegates in Congress to move that body to declare the colonies free and independent States;—signer of the Declaration of Independence, war governor of Virginia, and one of the most brilliant of that body of great men who stand, a splendid galaxy, in the firmament of our nation's history.

"The old store," which for two generations

yielded the Nelsons a harvest of golden guineas, stood on the open space now called "the common." It survived the siege, but was destroyed in the War of 1812. The custom-house, however, where their goods were entered, still stands a score of yards off, with moss-covered, peaked roof, thick walls, and massive oaken doors and shutters. This is one of the most notable relics of York, for it is said to have been one of the first custom-houses erected in America. In the colonial period, it was the fashionable rendezvous of the gentlemen of the town and surrounding country. There the young bucks in velvet and ruffles gathered to talk over the news or to plan new plots of surprising a governor or a lady-love. It was there that the haughty young aristocrats, as they took snuff and fondled their hounds, probably laughed over the story of how that young Washington, who had thought himself good enough for anybody, had courted pretty Mary Cary, and had been asked out of the house by the old colonel, on the ground that his daughter had been accustomed to ride in her own coach. There it was doubtless told how Tom Jefferson, leaving his clients and studies on the Rivanna, had come back to try his fate at Becky Burwell's dainty feet, and had been sent off for much-needed consolation to his old friend and crony, John Page, who had just induced little Frances, her cousin, to come and be mistress of Rosewell. Sometimes graver topics were discussed there; as, whether the Metropolitan's license and the recommendation of the governor were sufficient to override the will of the vestries in fixing an obnoxious rector in the parishes; whether Great Britain had a right to a monopoly of the colonial trade, or whether she could lawfully prevent them inhibiting the landing of slaves in their ports, with other questions which showed the direction of the popular mind.

It would be difficult to find a fitter illustration of the old colonial Virginia life than that which this little town affords. It was a typical Old Dominion borough, and was one of the eight boroughs into which Virginia was originally divided. One or two families owned the place, ruling with a sway despotic in fact, though in the main temperate and just, for the lower orders were too dependent and inert to dream of thwarting the "gentlefolk," and the Southerner when uncrossed was ever the most amiable of men. If there were more than one great family, they nevertheless got on amicably, for they had usually intermarried until their interests were identical.

Nearly all the "old" families in the colony were allied, and the clannish instinct was as strong as among the Scotch. The ambition of the wealthy families in the colony, perhaps more than the usually accepted aristocratic instinct, excluded from the circle all who did not come up to their somewhat difficult standard. Government was their passion, and everything relating to it interested them. It was the only matter which excited them, and every other feeling took its tone from this. It influenced them in all their relations, domestic as well as public. Even and smooth as seemed the temperament of the nonchalant, languid Virginian,—not splenitive or rash,—yet had it in it something dangerous. His political opinions were sacred to him; he had inherited them from his father, whom he regarded as the impersonation of wisdom and virtue. To oppose them roused him at once, and made him intolerant and violent. He could not brook opposition. The feeling has not altogether disappeared even at the present day. Yet, singular as it may seem, with this existed the deeply ingrained love of liberty and devotion to principle from which sprang the constitutional securities of liberty of speech, freedom of the press, the right to bear arms, and the statute of religious freedom.

In York, the Nelson family was the acknowledged leader in county affairs. President Nelson had sent his eldest son, Tom, when a lad of fourteen, to Eton, where he was a desk-mate of Charles James Fox, and afterward to Cambridge, where he was graduated with some distinction. The style in which the president of the Council lived is exhibited by the casual remark, in a letter written to a friend who was in charge of this son, that he had just bought Lord Baltimore's six white coach-horses, and meant to give his own six black ones a run in his Hanover pastures. In 1761, the young squire came home; and it shows the influence of his family that, while yet on his voyage across, he was returned as a member of the House of Burgesses. About a year afterwards, he married Lucy Grymes, the eldest daughter of Colonel Philip Grymes, of Brandon, in Middlesex. The Grymeses enjoyed the reputation of being the cleverest family in the Dominion. Little Lucy was a cousin of Light-Horse Harry Lee and of Thomas Jefferson. An old MS. states that the latter was one of her many lovers, but the story appears to lack confirmation, as the lady denied it even in after years.

During the years that followed, York maintained her position as an influential borough in the direction of affairs. When the crisis came, Secretary Thomas Nelson, "the President's" younger brother, was at the head of the moderate party. He received in the Convention forty-five votes for Virginia's first governor, but was beaten by Patrick Henry. He was, however, put in the Privy Council. The Marquis de Chastillux gives a pretty picture of the old gray-haired gentleman being brought out of York under a flag of truce by his two sons, officers in Washington's army. His nephew and namesake, Thomas Nelson, Jr., was one of the leaders of the ultra patriots, and with his cousin and connection, Dudley Digges, took so conspicuous a part in the early revolutionary action of the State, that Captain Montague, the commander of the British ship *Fowey,* threatened to bombard York. The manifestation of the Virginians' anger took a singular turn, which at the same time shows the naïve character of the old Virginia gentry. They solemnly resolved that this officer's action had been so inhuman that he should not be further recognized as a gentleman.

It is possible that however determined the men were not to recognize Captain Montague, the women were less resolute, as he was remarkable for his great personal beauty,—so remarkable, indeed, that it was said Lord Dunmore's daughter, Lady Augusta Murray, who afterward married the Duke of Sussex, and who was herself declared to be the handsomest woman in the three kingdoms, used to repeat at the end of each verse in the 136th Psalm, whenever it occurred in the church service:

> Praise Montague, Captain of the *Foweey*,
> For his beauty endureth forever.

Dudley Digges, young Nelson's colleague in the House of Burgesses, was a member of the Privy Council, and of the Committee of Safety. He was the worthy lineal descendant of that brave Sir Dudley who flung at Charles the First's powerful and insolent favorite, Buckingham, the retort, "Do you jeer, my lord? I can show you where a greater man than your lordship, as high in power, and as deep in the king's favor, has been hanged for as small a crime as these articles contain."

Such was York, the patriotic little Virginia

town into which Cornwallis retired in the summer of 1781, when he received orders from Sir Henry Clinton to intrench himself on the coast and await instructions. At this time it boasted among its citizens the governor of the State, for young Nelson had attained the highest dignity in Virginia. He had been one of the leaders in the great movement which had separated the colonies from the mother country. He had been a conspicuous member of all the great conventions. He had made the motion in committee of the whole in May, 1776, that Virginia should instruct her delegates in Congress to try and induce that body to declare the United Colonies free and independent States; he had himself carried this instruction to Philadelphia; he had, as one of Virginia's delegates, signed the great Declaration; and now he had been chosen to take the chief control of the State, and, with almost dictatorial powers, to manage both her military and civil polity. ''His popularity was unbounded,'' says the historian. Certainly his patriotism was. The father of a modern English statesman, speaking of his son's free-trade views, said he might be exalting the nation, but he was ruining his family. The same criticism might have been passed on General Nelson's administration. His patriotism was of a nature that now strikes one as rather antique. When money was wanted to pay the troops and run the government, Virginia's credit was low, but the governor was told that he could have plenty on his personal security, so he borrowed the sum needed, and went on; when regiments mutinied and refused to march, the governor simply drove over to Petersburg, raised the money on his individual credit, and paid them off. Consequently, when the war closed, what old George Mason declared he would be willing to say his *nunc dimittis* on, viz. the heritage to his children of a crust of bread and liberty, had literally befallen Governor Nelson.

When it was discovered that Cornwallis was marching on York, the feelings of the inhabitants were doubtless not enviable. Arnold had not long before swept over the State, with a traitor's rancor, leaving red ruin in his track. Colonel Tarleton, Cornwallis's lieutenant, had procured for himself a not very desirable reputation, having an eye for a good horse and a likely negro, and a conscience not over-scrupulous about the manner of obtaining them. Arnold was so much dreaded that, when he was expected to fall on York, Mrs. Nelson, the general's wife, with her young children, fled to the upper country. On this occasion it was that Jimmy Ridout, the carriage driver, in emulation of Cacus, had his horses shod at night with the shoes reversed, so that if they were followed their pursuers might be misled. When Cornwallis marched on York, Mrs. Nelson once more set out for her upper plantations in Hanover.

Cornwallis, expecting additional forces from Sir Henry Clinton, fortified himself in York. His letter to his chief, conveying the announcement of his surrender, declares that he never saw this post in a very favorable light, and nothing but the hope of relief would have induced him to attempt its defence. This letter gave mortal offence to the superior officer, who was sensible of the justice of the grave charge so delicately conveyed. He had sacrificed his subordinate and the last chances of Great Britain.

Strolling over the green fields at present, it requires an effort to picture the scenes they witnessed one hundred years ago. There are fortifications still standing, green with blackberry bushes and young locusts, but they tell of a more recent strife; the Revolutionary earthworks have totally disappeared, except on

"Secretary's Hill," where formerly stood Secretary Nelson's fine house, in which Cornwallis first established his headquarters. A few signs are still discernible there, due to the possible fact that his lordship had his headquarters protected by works of unusual strength. If this be the explanation, the precaution proved futile, for when it was known in the Revolutionary camp that it was the British commander's headquarters, the house was made their special mark, and was almost demolished. The butler was killed in the act of placing a dish on the dinner-table.

Outside the town, there are several spots which may be accurately fixed. Up the river, on the rise beyond the small, dull stream, to the left of the Williamsburg road going out, were posted the French batteries—the regiments of Touraine, Agénois, and Gatinois—the Royal Auvergne—"*Auvergne sans tache.*" On the creek, a little nearer the town, fell Scammel on the first day of the siege, treacherously shot in the back after he had surrendered, which "cast a gloom over the camp." His death was avenged afterward by his troops, as they charged over the redoubts with the battle-cry, "Remember Scammel!" Below the town, on the other side, the redoubts were stormed and taken at night by the picked troops of the French and American armies. The short grass now grows smooth over the spot where the Royal Auvergne won back their lost name and fame; but as we stand where they stood that night with empty guns, panting to use the bayonet, steadfast though their ranks were being mowed down in the darkness, we feel stirred as though it had all occurred but yesterday. Meantime the American stormers of the other redoubt, led by the dashing young Colonel Alexander Hamilton, had plunged through the abatis and gained their prize. What a speech that must have been which the young officer made his men as he halted them under the walls!

"Did you ever hear such a speech?" asked one officer of another. "With that speech I could storm hell!"

The striking incidents of the siege were not very numerous. It was a steady and unreceding advance on one side and retrogression on the other; but this particular night was somewhat noted for its romantic episodes. When Hamilton, arrived inside his redoubt, sent to inform the French leader of the other storming party of the fact and to inquire if he was in his, "No,

243

but I will be in five minutes,'' he answered, and he kept his word. Many a blue lapel was stained with heart blood; but their king wrote with his own hand, *"Bon pour Royal Auvergne,"* and posterity says, Amen! They died not in vain. "The work is done and well done,'' said Washington, when the signal was given that the redoubts were won.

A few days before this eventful night, the governor of Virginia, who was present in person, commanding the Virginia State forces, had displayed his patriotism by an act which attracted much attention. Observing that his own house within the town had escaped injury from the shells, he learned that General Washington had given orders that the gunners should not aim at it. He immediately had a gun turned on it, and offered a prize of five guineas to the gunner who should strike it.

Three-quarters of a mile back of the two captured redoubts, and outside of the first parallel, stood, and still stands, an old weather-board and weather-stained mansion. Its antique roof, its fireplaces set across the corners, and its general old-time air, even a hundred years ago, bespoke for it reverence as a relic of a long bygone age. It was historical even then, for it had been the country residence of Governor Spottswood, who had been the great Marlborough's aide-de-camp, and the best royal governor of the colony. He had come, bringing his virtues and his graces, to the Old Dominion, and had in the quaint old house on the river bank held his mimic court, forming royal plans for the development of the kingly domain he ruled, entertaining his knights of the Golden Horseshoe, drinking healths which amaze even this not over temperate generation. He established the first iron foundry ever erected on American soil.

Hither his body was brought from Maryland, where he died. But one hundred years ago, to the many associations connected with the old house was added one which to this generation dwarfs all others. In its sitting-room were drawn up the articles of capitulation of the British army, by which was ended the strife, and the colonies became free and independent States. Imagination almost always paints in high colors the scene of any great act in the world's drama, but a milder and more peaceful picture can scarcely be conceived than that which this spot now presents. The house was owned at the time of the surrender by Mrs. Moore, "Aunt Moore," as she was called by nearly all the people of York. It is now unoccupied, and the cellar has been utilized as a stable. About it the mild-eyed Alderneys browse the white clover, or gaze sleepily at the unwonted pilgrim. The river sleeps just beyond, in the summer sunshine, with a single white sail set like a pearl on its bosom. The spot looks an ''ancient haunt of peace,'' but war has stalked about it since first the English came. The peaceful-looking hedges beyond the old orchard, and on the bluff, are breastworks overgrown with bushes. The great Civil War, the War of 1812, and the Revolution, all have passed over these green, quiet fields; and yonder in the ''Temple'' lies the relic of a still older strife—the grave of a soldier who had won his laurels and lain down his sword long before Sir Alexander Spottswood earned his spurs at Blenheim. A mystery of more ancient date than the Revolution hangs about the spot, and is associated with the name. Some authorities state that Governor Spottswood built a temple of worship here, whence came the name of the plantation, ''Temple Farm''; but the Temple is doubtless of older date than this account would make us believe. The more probable explanation is that the building, whose foundations alone remain at present, was erected in the early days of the colony. The double walls, one within the other, give credit to the story that it was so built for defence against the Indians, and the date on Major Gooch's tomb, October, 1655, corroborates it. The tomb of the royal governor has long since disappeared. A fragment of Major Gooch's epitaph remains. It reads:

> Within this tomb there doth interred lie,
> No shape but substance, true nobility,
> Itself though young in years, just twenty-nine,
> Yet grac'd with virtues morall and divine,
> The church from him did good participate.
> In counsell rare fit to adorn a state.

Could the young soldier have had a fitter resting-place or a better epitaph?

Right below the Temple sleeps Wormley's Creek, with its myriad water-lilies resting on its tranquil breast; and not a hundred yards above stands the modern successor to the mill, where the first shot in the siege was fired. The old structure has disappeared, but the old customs still remain. Here, twice a week, on Tuesdays and Fridays (for it takes three days to "catch a head of water"), come the negroes and country folk, bringing their "turns" of corn, some in bags on their heads, or, if they are of larger means and appetites, in little carts with generally a single bull harnessed in the shafts. The established rule of "each in his turn" prevails, and they wait patiently, sometimes the livelong day, until their time comes. They are not in a hurry; for a hundred years this same life has gone on as placid and serene as the stream down among the "cow collards"; to hurry would be to violate the most ancient and time-honored tradition of the fathers.

It is easy to see that "Little York" never recovered from its bombardment. The scene in the street to-day is an idyl,—a few massive old brick houses scattered among modern shanties like so many old-time gentlemen at a modern ward-meeting; a couple of negro children kicking up the dust in the street a hundred yards away; two citizens sitting under an awning "resting," and a small ox-cart moving uncertainly nearer, as the little brindled bull in the shafts browses the short grass on the side of the street. The most lively things in sight are a small boy and the string of fish he is carrying; for the latter have just come from the water and are still fluttering. Such is the scene now presented in the street where a hundred years ago anxious red-coats double-quicked along or stole sullenly by, trying to shelter themselves from the searching messengers from the batteries out on the heights beyond the creeks.

The Nelson house still remains in the family; but to the Nelsons, peace came with poverty; the governor's vast estate went for his public debts. He gave the whole of it. When a question arose in the Virginia Convention as to the confiscation of British claims, he stopped the agitation by rising in his seat, and declaiming, "Others may do as they please; but as for me, I am an honest man, and so help me God! I will pay my debts." Years afterward, Virginia did tardy and partial justice to the memory of Nelson's great services by placing his statue among the group of her great ones in her beautiful Capital Square; and, in company with Washington, Jefferson, Marshall, Henry, Mason, and Lewis, he stands in bronze tendering the bonds with his outstretched hands, *in perpetuam rei memoriam*. No recompense, however, was ever made to the family for the vast sums Governor Nelson had expended, and his widow, once the wealthiest woman in the colony, was left blind in her old age, with only one piece of property, her children's mammy. Some forty or fifty years after his death, evidence of his great losses was collected for the purpose of applying to Congress for compensation; but a bill being brought in meantime for the relief of the widow of the young colonel who made the speech to his storming party that night under the walls of the redoubt at Yorktown, and who had rendered besides some other small services to the country, a member asked if there were no poorhouses in New York, that Mrs. Hamilton came begging to Congress; and after that, one of Governor Nelson's sons, who was in Congress at the time, refused to proceed further in the matter, declaring that he would not permit his mother's name to be brought before a body which tolerated such a speech.

It seems extraordinary that, after only a hundred years, much doubt exists as to the actual spot where the British laid down their arms. Immediately after the surrender, Congress enacted that a suitable monument should be erected there, to tell the story to succeeding generations. But all things concerning Yorktown sleep, and the memorial was neglected until the very spot was forgotten. There was built up, however, a mighty nation, zealous for liberty,

TWO OLD COLONIAL PLACES

Monumentum aere perennius
Regalique situ pyramidum altius.

This was, to use the closing words of the articles of Cornwallis's capitulation, "done in the trenches before Yorktown, in Virginia, October 19th, 1781."

II.

AS York, the territory of the Nelsons, witnessed the last act in Virginia's colonial drama, so Rosewell, the seat of the Pages, saw the first act. The places are only a few miles apart, but are separated by the York River.

Taking a small boat at the Yorktown pier, you may, by promising an extra quarter, wake the lethargic boatman into positive activity, and get under way to Gloucester Point in something under a half-hour. Your boatman, as black as Charon, rows with a deliberation which would gratify you if crossing the Styx. You are apt to question him about the surrender. Oh, yes! he knows all about it. If his immediate predecessor, "Old Unc' Felix," who was gathered last fall to his fathers at the age of sixty-five years, and whose funeral sermon was preached last Sunday, were alive, he would have assured you that he remembered all about the siege of Yorktown, and waited on both Generals Washington and Cornwallis.

After a while you reach Gloucester Point, literally a "point," and tread the ground invested by Weedon, De Choisy, and the dashing, bragging De Lauzun.

A ride of a few miles up the river bank brings you to an old place called Shelly, once a part of the Rosewell estate, and still owned by Governor Page's descendants. However appropriate the name may seem, in view of the great beds of shell down on the river bank, it does not call up the associations connected with the name borne by the place in colonial days—"Werowocomoco." Next to Jamestown, this plantation is perhaps the spot most celebrated in the colonial annals of Virginia. It was here that Powhatan reigned like Egbert of old, with kings, less poetic but not more savage, to pull his canoe. Between his wives, his enemies, and his English friends, the old Werowance had a hard time. Doubtless he found much consolation in his oysters. And judging from the mounds of oyster-shells, those Indians must have had royal appetites. It was at this place that the most romantic incident of Virginia's history occurred, when the little tender-hearted Indian maiden, touched with pity for an intrepid young captive, prayed in vain for his life, and then flung herself beneath the executioner's axe and clasped the victim in her arms, risking her own life, but saving John Smith and the colony of Virginia.

Other memories cluster around the place: of the ghastly decorations of Payanketank scalps; the ballet dance of Indian nymphs attired in the most ancient of recorded costumes; the coronation of old Powhatan, who with royal instinct refused to stoop while the crown was placed on his head. The whole place is quick with memories.

It has always been my opinion that the world has not done justice to Captain John Smith. He deserves to be ranked with the greatest explorers of all time. At the age of thirty he had left the Virginias and returned to England, having accomplished what Raleigh, with all his wealth, power, and zeal, could not do. Well might the old chronicles call him "the Father of the Colony." Had the die turned differently on the spot where we now stand, Virginia might have lain a hundred years more a wilderness and a waste place, and the destinies of the world have been different. Until a few years ago one might have said of "oure Captaine" as the Spartan said to a Sophist offering to deliver a eulogy on Hercules—"Why, who has ever blamed Hercules?" But of late the wise critics have attacked him virulently. Here, however, is what was said of him by one who had shared his dangers:

"What shall I say but thus; we lost him that in all his proceedings made justice his first guide and experience his second, ever hating baseness, sloath, pride and indignitie more than any dangers; that never allowed more for himselfe than his souldiers with him; that upon no dangers would send them where he would not lead them himselfe; that would never see vs want what he either had, or could by any means get vs; that would rather want then borrow, or starve then not pay; that loved action more then words, and hated falshood and covetousness worse than death; whose adventures were our lives, and whose losse our deaths."

A few miles below here on the bluff stands Powhatan's Chimney, the sole remaining relic of the royalty of the old Indian king. It stood until a few years ago, when owing to our shameful neglect of all things historical, it fell and now it lies prone. It had the honor of being built by Captain Smith, and was erected on the requisition of the Emperor for ''a house, a grind-stone, fifty swords, some guns, a cock and hen, with much copper and *many beads.*'' The fireplace is wide enough to roast an ox, and there is grave suspicion that it has served to roast other cattle—Payanketank rebels and the like. All this land about here was a part of the old Page estate, Rosewell. Away to the left it stretches, taking in all of Timber Neck, which came to the Pages in 1690 with Mary Mann, whom Matthew Page married.

That broad stream down there is Carter's Creek. There it was that Powhatan and his people used to land in pre-colonial days, and brown canoes, driven by dark warriors or dusky maidens, shot in and out. Later on, in the spring evenings, white-winged sailboats, with proud-faced dames and portly, ruddy gentlemen, or with laughing girls in rich attire, and gay young gallants, glided to and fro, now drifting wide apart, now near together, side by side, amid mirth and shouts and laughter.

Across the creek, a hundred yards, stands Rosewell, the ancient Page mansion, massive, stark, and lonely, a solid cube of ninety feet. Once it had long colonnades and ample wings, the ruins of which latter yet stand, and it was

256

flanked by great and numerous out-buildings—
stables, barns, warehouses, and negro quarters.
All have vanished before the years, and nothing
is left except the stately old mansion.

When it was built in 1725-30, it was the
largest mansion in Virginia, and continued such
for many years. Indeed, there are but few as
large now. The great hall was wainscoted with
mahogany, and the balustrade of the grand
stairway, also of mahogany, was beautifully
carved by hand to represent baskets of fruit,
flowers, etc. The roof over the windows was
originally covered with lead, but during the
Revolution it was stripped off for bullets by its
master, the fiery patriot, John Page, who
presented the lead to the State and was hardly
persuaded at last to receive for it even conti-
nental money. The letter of Edmund Pendleton
regarding it is still in existence. The master of
Rosewell came out of the war with broken fortunes, his large plantations going one after another to pay his debts. Shortly after his death,
the place was sold for twelve thousand dollars
to a man, who after making a fortune by selling
everything he could sell, from the trees on the
lawn to the wainscoting in the hall, sold the
place, stripped and denuded as it was, at a large

advance. The vandal not only sold the bricks around the graveyard, and the fine old cedars in the avenue, but what was even worse, white-washed the superb carved mahogany wainscoting and balustrade. Once again it is in the hands of gentlefolk.

There is a tradition that Thomas Jefferson, while absent from his seat in Congress in 1775-76, spent some time at this house, in reflection and study, crystallizing into worthy expression those principles which he was shortly afterward to set forth in the "Great Declaration." It is said that he then submitted his rough draft of that great paper to his friend John Page before it was seen by any one else, and when independence was no more than a possibility. There was then a summer-house on the roof, and the place where it stood is pointed out as the spot where the paper was read and discussed. There is, perhaps, nothing to substantiate the legend, except that it has always been one of the traditions of the house.

The founder of the Page family in Virginia was "Collonel John Page," who, thinking that a principality in Utopia might prove better than an acre in Middlesex, where he resided, came over in 1656. He came from the pretty little village of Bedfont, Middlesex, where the Pages had for generations been lords of the small manor of Pate, and where they lie buried in the chancel of the quaint little Norman church. He was a literary man, and in his latter days wrote a book of religious meditations which he dedicated to his son. It was entitled "A Deed of Gift," and is written in the quaint and earnest style of the seventeenth century. It shows him to have been a man of no mean ability and of deep piety. He gave the land on which is built the old church in Williamsburgh, and a fragment of his tombstone recording his virtues used to lie across the walk doing service as a paving flag until a few years ago, when it was removed by a pious descendant to the interior of the church, and a monument was erected to his memory. He had an eye for "bottom-land," and left his son Matthew an immense landed estate, which he dutifully increased by marrying Mary Mann, the rich heiress of Timber Neck. Their son, Mann, was a lad thirteen years old when his father died. After being sent to Eton, he came back and took his place at the "Council Board," as his fathers had done before him and his descendants did after him.

Mann Page built the Rosewell mansion. The

bricks and material were all brought from England, and the stately pile grew slowly under the Virginia sun to be a marvel of pride and beauty for that time. The long inscription upon the tomb "piously erected to his memory by his mournfully surviving lady" presents a complete biography of Mann, who, together with his pride, possessed the independence, the dignity, and the virtue so often found combined in the old colonial gentleman. He possessed the colonial instinct, and fought the tax which the home government wished to place on tobacco. The tradition is that he died just as he completed the mansion, and that the first time the house was used was when his body was laid out in the great hall. The three surviving sons of Mann were Mann, John, and Robert, who became the heads respectively of the Rosewell, the North End, and the Broadneck branches of the family. Mann's eldest son, John, was a most ardent patriot, and would undoubtedly have been hanged if General Washington had surrendered to Cornwallis, instead of the latter to him. He and Thomas Jefferson were at William and Mary College together, and that closest of bonds, a college friendship, commenced there and lasted throughout their lives. As college students, they together stood at the door of the House of Burgesses, and, looking in, heard Patrick Henry ring out his famous warning to George III. From that time, the two young men were rebels, and their views were of the most advanced order. There remain a number of rattling "college-boy" letters which passed between the cronies at a time when the light of the world, to them, were "Nancy's" and "Belinda's" eyes, and Fame's siren voice had not sounded in their ears. In a letter bearing date Christmas Day, 1762, Jefferson, frozen up in his Albemarle home, wrote his friend:

"You cannot conceive the satisfaction it would give me to have a letter from you. Write me circumstantially everything which happened at the wedding. Was she there? Because, if she was, I ought to have been at the devil for not being there too."

The "she" alluded to was his lady-love, Miss Rebecca Burwell. The letter goes on:

"Tell Miss Alice Corbin that I verily believe the rats knew I was to win a pair of garters from her, or they never would have been so cruel as to carry mine away. This very consideration makes me so sure of the bet that I shall ask everybody I see from that part of the world

what pretty gentleman is making his addresses
to her. I would fain ask Miss Becca Burwell to
give me another watch paper of her own cutting,
which I should esteem much more, though it
were a plain round one, than the nicest in the
world cut by other hands.''

A few weeks later, he writes to his friend a
mournful, woeful epistle, like that of any other
lovelorn swain. After inveighing against the
dullness of his life, he says:

''How have you done since I saw you? How
did Nancy look at you when you danced with her
at Southall's? Have you any glimmering of
hope? How does R. B. do? Had I better stay
here and do nothing, or go down and do less?
Or, in other words, had I better stay here while
I am here or go down, that I may have the pleasure of sailing up the river again in a full-rigged
flat? Inclination tells me to go, receive my sentence, and be no longer in suspense; but reason
says, if you go, and your attempt proves unsuccessful, you will be ten times more wretched
than ever.... I hear that Ben Harrison has
been to Wilton. Let me know his success.''

Ben Harrison's success at Wilton, where he
was courting Anne Randolph, a cousin of both
Jefferson and Page, was greater than that of

either the writer of the letter with "R. B." or of the recipient with "Nancy." Miss Anne, after leading her lover a reasonable dance, married him, and had the honor of being the wife of a governor of Virginia. "Nancy" and "Little Becky" might themselves have sat in even higher places than they did sit in had they only smiled a little more on their lovers. Cupid, however, lacks the gift of prophecy; and Fame will not tell her secrets till the time comes, for the sweetest lips that ever smiled.

Young Page, having failed with Nancy, found consolation at the feet of his sweet cousin, Frances Burwell, daughter of Colonel Burwell of Carter's Creek, and the niece of President and Secretary Nelson. When quite a young man he became a member of the King's Council and of the Board of Trustees of the College, and represented that institution in the General Assembly.

When the storm came, Page, although the youngest member of the King's Council, was the head of the Republican element in the Council. He represented Gloucester in the Great Convention, was elected president of the Privy Council, and was a member of the Committee of Safety that had control of the Virginia forces. He served as a colonel in the army. He was also a member of the first Congress, and continued a representative from Virginia for eight years, and until, as he said, John Adams and Alexander Hamilton shut him out.

He was a man of great culture as well as of large wealth. His classical library was probably as fine as any in the colonies; and he was, for his time, a man of scientific attainments. His calculations of eclipses still exist, and it indicates the spirit of the period, that he made them not for Virginia, but "for Rosewell." He was a stanch Republican, and the selection of Virginia's famous motto, *Sic Semper Tyrannis,* and of the figure of Liberty on our coin was due to him.

Like their kinsmen, the Nelsons, the Pages were Episcopalians, living after the straitest sect of their religion so strictly that they were regarded as the pillars of the establishment in the colony. Yet, great as was their love for the Church, their love of liberty was not less, and they took an active part in the disestablishment. The purity of their motives will be understood when it is learned that the families were such rigid churchmen that Mrs. General Nelson never was in a "meeting-house" in her life, and never heard a "dissenter" preach, except when, being present with her husband in Philadelphia, in July, 1776, her patriotism overcame her principles, and she went to hear Doctor Witherspoon preach before Congress.

John Page was a great churchman, and was urged to stand for orders and take the Virginia mitre when it was first decided to send a bishop to the colony, but he declined. The importunity of his friends at length worried him so, that he said "he 'd be damned if he would be their bishop"—a resolution this expression of which probably saved him further trouble on that score.

After the Revolution, the master of Rosewell became governor of Virginia, and continued to be re-elected until, after three terms, he became ineligible by constitutional limitation.

So long as the master lived, Rosewell, although mortgaged for debts contracted for the cause of liberty, was kept up, a grand old Virginia mansion, open to all, gentle and simple, the home of hospitality more boundless than the wealth of all its owners. But after that it passed out of the family. It is, perhaps, the most interesting, as it is the largest, colonial relic in the South.

THE OLD SOUTH

The following sketch of Colonel John Page of Rosewell, sometime governor of the Commonwealth of Virginia, was written by him in the form of a letter to Skelton Jones, Esq., of Richmond, Virginia. It was in answer to one which was addressed to Colonel Page, dated August, 1808, submitting certain queries concerning his life, character, etc., and requesting him to give answers thereto, which might be embodied in a narrative, and published in a work which Mr. Jones was about to issue from the press, probably the continuation of Burke's "History of Virginia."

I was born on the 17th day of April, old style, Anno Domini, 1743, at Rosewell. I discover from the tomb stones in Williamsburg Churchyard, and from others in my Grandfather's burying ground, at his family seat, Rosewell, 1st, that one of my ancestors named John Page, was a highly respectable character, and had long been one of the King's Council in this Colony, when he died, viz. on the 23d January, 1691-2; his manuscripts which I have seen, prove that he was learned and pious. 2d. That his Son Matthew Page was one of the Council, and his Son Mann also, whose letters to his friends, and theirs to him, exhibit as a patriotic, well educated, and truly amiable gentleman. He had his classical education at Eton school in England. He was my father's father, who might also have been appointed to the office of a Councillor, but he declined it in favour of his younger brother John Page, who, my father said, having been brought up in the study of the law regularly, was a much more proper person for that office than he was. The John Page above first mentioned was, as we find by an old picture, a Sir John Page, a merchant of London, supposed to have been knighted, as Sir John Randolph long after was, for proposing a regulation of the Tobacco trade and a duty thereon. Which if it was the case, I think his patriotism was premature, and perhaps misplaced; his dear, pure-minded, and American patriotic grandson, my grandfather, Mann Page, in his days checked the British Merchants from claiming even freight on their goods from England, declaring that their freight on our Tobacco, and homeward bound articles, added to their monopoly of our Trade, ought to satisfy avarice itself: this he expressed repeatedly to his mercantile friends, and some near relations who were Tobacco merchants in London; however he lived not long after! The fashion or practice then was for men of landed property here, to dispose of their children in the following manner: they entailed all their lands on their eldest son, brought up their others, according to their genius and disposition, physicians, or lawyers, or merchants, or ministers of the church of England, which commonly maintained such as were frugal and industrious. My father was frequently urged by friends, but not relations, to pay court to Sir Gregory

Page, whose heir from his Coat of Arms, and many circumstances, he was supposed to be. But he despised titles sixty years ago, as much as you and I do now; and would have nothing to say to the rich silly Knight, who died, leaving his estate and title to a sillier man than himself, his sister's son, a Mr. Turner, on condition that he would take the name and title of Sir Gregory Page, which he did by act of Parliament, as I was told, or read.

I was early taught to read and write, by the care and attention of my grandmother, one of the most sensible, and best informed women I ever knew. She was a daughter of the Hon. Robert Carter, who was President of the King's Council, and Secretary of Virginia, and who at the same time, held the rich office of Proprietor of the Northern neck, by purchase, from the Lord Proprietor, his friend, who was contented to receive but 300*l.* per annum for it, as the report in the family stated. My Grandmother excited in my mind an inquisitiveness, which, whenever it was proper, she gratified, and very soon I became so fond of reading, that I read not only all the little amusing and instructing books which she put in my hands, but many which I took out of my father's and grandfather's collection, which was no contemptible library.

But in the year 1752, when I was nine years old, my father put me into a grammar school, at the glebe house of our parish, where the Rev'd Mr. Wm. Yates had undertaken the tuition of twelve scholars. I found there Lewis Willis (the late Col. L. W.) of

Frederickburg, Edward Carter, (his brother, Charles
Carter of Shirley, had just left this school and gone
to William and Mary College,) Severn Eyre, of the
Eastern Shore, Peter Beverley Whiting, and his
brother John, Thos. Nelson, (the late Gen. Nelson,)
Christopher Robinson of Middlesex, Augustine Cook,
and John Fox of Gloster; so that I made up, or
kept up the number which Yates required; but in
a short time, his passionate disposition induced L.
Willis, and Edward Carter to leave him, and Severn
Eyre not long after followed the Carters to our College, where Edward had joined his brother Charles.
The two Whitings followed them, and Mr. Nelson,
and Col. Tucker, took their sons and sent them to
England, to finish their education; and at the end
of my year, Robinson, Cooke, and Fox, went to College, and my father and Mr. Willis procured a most
excellent tutor for their sons, instead of sending
them there. I had been totally interrupted in my
delightful reading of Histories, and Novels, for
twelve months tied down to get by heart an insipid
and unintelligible book, called Lilly's Grammar, one
sentence in which my master never explained. But
happily, my new tutor Mr. Wm. Price, at Mr. Willis's, soon enabled me to see that it was a complete
Grammar, and an excellent key to the Latin Language. This faithful and ingenious young man, who
was about 20 years of age, and had been studying
the language at his leisure, as he was intended for
the church, into which he could not enter till he was
24 years of age, was happily of a most communi-

cative disposition, and possessed the happiest talents of explaining what he taught, and rendering it an agreeable, and most desirable object; was beloved and strictly attended to by me. After 3 years close application to my studies under Mr. Price, some circumstances occurred which induced him to accept of the office of Secretary to the Hon. Philip Ludwell, who was deputed by the Governor to meet a Convention of Governors, or their deputies, at New York, to resolve on the quotas of money that each colony should furnish to carry on the war against France, and his mind had been so inflamed by the military ardour displayed in the letters of Capt. George Mercer, (afterwards Colonel of the 2d Va. Regiment,) another old fellow collegian, who had quitted the academic groves there for the field of Mars, which he had always read to me with enthusiasm, that he resolved to abandon the humble employment he was in, and to fly to the Royal standard, to fight as it seemed necessary then to do, *pro Aris et Focis*, instead of going to England for a License to come back, and preach and pray. For Braddock's defeat had terrified all but the brave, and every coward believed and said that we were on the point of destruction. My dearly beloved Tutor, however, after having enjoyed Lieutenancy a few months in the British army, died!

It is highly probable that Mr. Price's Whiggish principles, and his inducing me to admire Roman and Grecian Heroes, and to delight in reading of wars and battles, and to enquire on what the success of those interesting events turned, "gave the colour and complexion" to my prospects and conduct through life; otherwise I know not what could have borne me up to defy the terrible threats of George the 3d, and at last actually oppose his troops in arms, as the heroical militia of Gloster, now Gloster and Mathews, enabled me to do.

After I had lost my tutor Mr. Price, my father entered me in the Grammar School at William and Mary College, when I was 13 years of age, instead of sending me to England, as he had promised my mother he would, before I should arrive at that age. But fortunately for me, several Virginians, about this time, had returned from that place (where we were told learning alone existed) so inconceivably illiterate, and also corrupted and vicious, that he swore no son of his should ever go there, in quest of an education. The most remarkable of these was his own Cousin Robert Carter, of Nominy, who however in a course of years, after he had got a seat at the Council board, studied Law, History, and Philosophy, and although his knowledge was very limited, and his mind confused by studying without the assistance of a tutor, he conversed a great deal with our highly enlightened Governor, Fauquier, and Mr. Wm. Small, the Professor of Mathematics at the College of Wm. and Mary, from whom he derived great advantages. And his understanding was so enlarged, that he discovered the cruel tyrannical designs of the British government, and when I found him at the Council Board, in the time of Lord

Dunmore, he was a pure and steady patriot. At College, as my father put me to lodge, board, &c., at the President's, Thomas Dawson, a younger brother of Dr. William Dawson, at whose death Thomas succeeded to his office of President of William and Mary College, and the Bishop of London's Commissary in Virginia, and of course became his successor in the Council; for the Bishop of London always had sufficient weight with the King, to place his Deputy Bishop, as we may call him, in that mimick deputy House of Lords—I say at College, as I lived with the President, who my Father had feed handsomely to be my private tutor, and he, finding me far better graduated in Latin than many boys much older than myself, was proud to introduce his pupil to the particular attention, first of Governor Dinwiddie, an old Scotch gentleman, who was fond of appearing a patron of learning, and secondly, to Governor Fauquier, to whose much greater learning and judgment my ever to be beloved Professor, Mr. Small, had held me up as worthy of his attention;—I had finished my regular course of studies, in the Philosophy Schools, after having gone through the Grammar School, before the death of Governor Fauquier; and having married Miss Frances Burwell, only daughter of the Hon. Robert Burwell, and of his wife Sarah Nelson, the half sister of William Nelson, and Thos. Nelson, (two brothers and members of the King's Council,) I was by these gentlemen, introduced to Lord Botetourt's attention, when he arrived here as Governor, and, after his death,

to Lord Dunmore, on his arrival. These circumstances contributed to introduce me into public life;
and added to my having been twice elected, by the
President and Professor of Wm. and Mary College,
to represent it in our general Assembly, and had
been appointed by the Governor and visitors, a visitor of the College.

As a visitor, I faithfully supported the rights and
privileges of both Professors and Students; and notwithstanding I had been placed at the Council
Board by Lord Dunmore, I opposed his nomination
of John Randolph as a visitor, boldly declaring that
as he had been rejected on a former occasion, as
not possessing the disposition and character, moral
and religious, which the Charter and Statutes of the
College required, he ought not again to be nominated,
till it could be proved that he had abandoned his
former principles, and practices, which no one
could venture to say he had. I then proposed Nathaniel Burwell, in the place of Lord Dunmore's nomination, and he was elected I think by every voice
except Dunmore's. For this, although he never
shewed any marks of resentment, I found I had incurred his displeasure, and that of his Secretary,
Capt. Edward Foy, who resented my conduct so
much before some of my friends, that I was obliged
to call him to an account for it—and he, like a brave
and candid man, made full reparation to me, and
my friend James Innes, at that time Usher of the
Grammar School in William and Mary College, afterwards the well-known Col. Innes. I continued to

discharge the duty of a visitor till I was elected a member of Congress, when finding that I could not attend the visitations, I resigned my office of visitor. As a member of the General Assembly, I voted always in favour of civil and religious liberty; that is for the enaction of those laws that would promote either, and for the abolition of entails. In the Council, I adhered to my former Whiggish principles, and of course opposed the Tory principles of the Governor, a pupil of Lord Bute; for he boasted that he was the companion of George III. during his tuition under that Earl—(*"Par nobile Fratrum!"*). At one Board, I joined with those patriotic members who advised the issuing of new writs for the election and call of an Assembly, and at a time when it was dangerous (as far as a loss of office went) to propose it, as the Governor had plainly given us to understand, that the King was determined to rule the Colonies without their check, or controul; and at another Board, I boldly advised the Governor to give up the Powder and Arms, which he had removed from the Magazine. But he flew into an outrageous passion, smiting his fist on the table, saying, "Mr. Page, I am astonished at you." I calmly replied I had discharged my duty, and had no other advice to give. As the other Councillors neither seconded or opposed me, he was greatly embarrassed. As I was never summoned to attend another Board, I might well suspect I was suspended from my office; but as I cared nothing about that, I never enquired whether I was or not.

P. Henry, afterwards so famous for his military parade against Dunmore, did actually bully him, but they appeared to me to be mutually afraid of each other. I never refused any office, however humble, or however perilous. I served as Col. of a Regiment of Militia, which was offered me during a serious invasion; and resigned but that of Councillor, after having served, as I expressed in my letter to the General Assembly, beyond what I conceived was the time contemplated by the Constitution.

In 1784, I served as an Academician, with Bishop Madison, Mr. R. Andrews, and Andrew Ellicott, in ascertaining and fixing the boundary between Pennsylvania and Virginia; and in 1785, as a Lay Deputy of the Protestant Episcopal Church, deputed by the Convention of Virginia with the Rev. Dr. Griffiths, and the Rev. Mr. McCroskey to represent—— in the Grand Convention, at New York. I then served my native county as a representative in Assembly, till the new Constitution threw me into Congress, where I served my country eight years with a safe conscience, till John Adams and A. Hamilton shut me out; I however repeatedly struggled to get in again, but in vain.

I would require volumes to describe what I did whilst in the Committee of Safety, Council, and Congress, and no small one to relate the interesting and hazardous services I performed with my brave associates in Gloster and Mathews. If I live my Memoirs shall do justice to the brave and patriotic county, Lieut. Peyton, and many others who deserve; but my Lieut. Col. Thomas Baytop, and his brave patriotic brother, who served under him freely during those times, and Capt. Camp, now Colonel, are alive, as is also Capt. Hudgins, now of Mathews, who displayed, with many other officers, bravery and skill, particularly Col. J. Baytop.

I next served in the military character as Lieut. Col. Commandant in Gloster and took my tour of duty, as Commander of a Regiment, composing part of the quota called from Virginia, to quell the insurgents in the Western Country. Though sick, I marched and joined my Brigadier at Winchester, and my Major General at Frankfort, near the foot of the Alleghany, who finding me actually ill, wrote me a consolatory letter, and advised me to return home by slow marches.

.   .   .   .

Before I had the benefit of a Philosophical education at College, with Mr. Jefferson, Mr. Walker, Dabney Carr, and others, under the illustrious Professor of Mathematics, Wm. Small, Esq., afterwards well known as the great Dr. Small, of Birmingham, the darling friend of Darwin, History, and particularly military and naval History, attracted my attention. But afterwards, natural and experimental Philosophy, Mechanics, and, in short, every branch of the Mathematics, particularly Algebra, and Geometry, warmly engaged my attention, till they led me on to Astronomy, to which after I had left College, till some time after I was married,

I devoted my time. I never thought, however, that
I had made any great proficiency in any study, for
I was too sociable, and fond of the conversation of
my friends to study as Mr. Jefferson did, who could
tear himself away from his dearest friends, to fly to
his studies.

The memoir was never completed, having
been interrupted by the illness and death of its
author. He succeeded James Monroe as governor of Virginia in 1802. This office he held
for three successive terms,—the longest period
allowed by the Constitution,—and was there-
after appointed by Mr. Jefferson Commissioner
of Loans for Virginia, which office he held at
the time of his death, on the 11th of October,
1808. In 1790, while a member of Congress, he
married his second wife, Miss Margaret
Lowther of New York, who survived him, as
did also children of each marriage.

He lies buried in the churchyard of "Old St.
John's,"[1] Richmond, Virginia, close to the walls
which he held sacred to the service of God and
his country.

[1]Here met on the 20th of March, 1775, the Second Virginia Convention, which lasted a week, and adjourned after taking steps
for putting the colony in a " posture of defence. " It was during
the debate on this subject that Patrick Henry made the famous
speech concluding with the well-known sentence, " Give me
liberty, or give me death!"

THE OLD VIRGINIA LAWYER

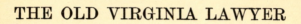

THE OLD VIRGINIA LAWYER

I KNEW him only in his latter days; but I have known those who knew him well, and thus I have come to have some knowledge of him; and as he has passed away it seems to me well that some memory of him should be preserved. He was a notable personage; a character well worth preserving; a constituent part of our civilization. He was the most considerable man of the county. The planter, the preacher, and the doctor were all men of position and consideration; but the old lawyer surpassed them all. Without the wealth of the planter, the authority of the clergyman, or the personal affection which was the peculiar possession of the family physician, the old lawyer held a position in the county easily first. He was, indeed, as has been aptly said, a planter, though he was not that primarily. Primarily he was a lawyer. He managed his farm only by the way.

Often, perhaps generally, he was of good family and social connection; or, if he was not, he was a man of such native force of mind and character that he had made and maintained his position without such adventitious aids, in a social system to the aristocratic exclusiveness of which his case was the single exception. Generally, he was both clever and ambitious; for only the exceptionally clever and ambitious were put at the bar.

He had the prestige of a college education (except in the instance mentioned, where by his natural powers he had, without such aid, made himself), and his education was an education indeed, not a mere cramming of the memory with so many facts or so many statements concerning so many things. His knowledge was not *rudis indigestaque moles*.

Thus when he left college he had a mind trained to work on whatever was before it, like a well-adjusted machine, and not a mere shell littered up with indiscriminate information. He was ambitious, and his aspirations were high; otherwise he would not have taken to the bar. Probably he had taken a turn at politics as a young man, usually on the losing side. If he was successful, he generally continued in politics, and thus was not an "old lawyer," but a statesman or politician who might or might not practise law by the way.

His training was not always that of the modern law-class; but it was more than a substitute for it; and it was of its own kind, complete. He "read law under" some old lawyer, some friend of his father or himself, who, although not a professor, was, without professing it, an admirable teacher. He associated with him constantly, in season and out of season; he saw him in his every mood; he observed him in intercourse with his clients, with his brothers of the bar, with the outside world; he heard him discourse of law, of history, of literature, of religion, of philosophy; he learned from him to ponder every manifestation of humanity; to consider the great underlying principles into which every proposition was resolvable; he found in him an exemplification of much that he inculcated, and a frank avowal of that wherein he failed. He learned to accept Lord Coke's dictum: *"melior est petere fontes quam sectari rivulos,"*—to look to the sources rather than to tap the streams; he fed upon the strong meat of the institutes and, the commentaries, with the great leading cases which stand now as principles; he received by absorption the traditions of the profession. On these, like a healthy child, he grew strong without taking note. Thus in due time when his work came he was fully equipped. His old tutor had not only taught him law; he had taught him that the law was a science, and a great, if not the greatest science.

He had impressed him with the principles which he himself held, and they were sound; he had, indeed, stamped upon his mind the conviction that he, his tutor, was the greatest lawyer of his time, a conviction which no subsequent observation nor experience ever served to remove.

His law library was a curious one; it embraced the great text-writers, only the greatest —Bracton, Coke upon Littleton, Blackstone— generally in old editions with marginal notes in the handwriting of his early and ambitious days; it had probably the Virginia Reports and a few, a very few, old English reports, the decisions of Lord Hardwicke and Lord Mansfield being among them, generally in odd volumes, the others having been borrowed and never returned.

On circuit he carried his library and his wardrobe in his saddle-bags.

If, however, his law library was scant, his general library was much more complete; on the shelves of his book-presses were the classics, both Latin and English, all testifying use, for nothing there was for show. These he knew; he not only read them, but loved them; he associated with them; he revelled in them. The poets and sages of the past were his teachers, his friends.

He had made his mark, perhaps unexpectedly, in some case in which the force of his maturing intellect had suddenly burst forth, astonishing alike the bar and the bench, and enrapturing the public. Perhaps it was a criminal case; perhaps one in which equity might be on his side, with the law dead against him; and which was regarded by older men with the conservatism of age as impossible until, by his brilliant effort, he unexpectedly won it. As like as not he rode forty miles that night to give a flower to his sweetheart.

From this time his reputation, his influence, and his practice increased. His professional position was henceforth assured. He had risen from a tyro to be an old lawyer.

He married early, and for love, the daughter of a gentleman, very likely of the old lawyer with whom he had read law; perhaps a beauty and a belle, who, with many suitors, chose the young lawyer, whom older men were beginning to speak of, and younger men were already following; who had brought her the news of his victory that night, and who could cope with her father in a discussion or disdainfully destroy a younger disputant. He took her to live on some poor plantation, in an old house which stood amid great oaks and hickories, with scanty furniture and few luxuries, yet which, under their joint influence, became an old Virginia home, and a centre of hospitality and refinement. Here he *lived,* not merely had his being, a machine or part of a machine; but lived, and what a life it was! The body fed and kept in health; the soul free from vice and debasement, dwelling in constant intercourse with a beautiful being; in communion, if not with God, at least with his two chief ministers: Nature and a gracious, gentle, and pure woman; the intellect nourished by association with a pure spirit, by contact with the best thought of ancient and modern times, and by constant and philosophic reflection. The world prospered; friends surrounded him; young children with their mother's eyes came and played about his feet, with joyous voices making his heart content. Thus he grew, his circle ever widening as the circle of our horizon widens when we climb towards heaven. These were some of the influences which created him.

Let me mention one of the chief. It was his wife. She believed in him; she worshipped him. She knew he ought to be Chief Justice of the United States. She was the supreme presence which made his home and gave him in large part his distinctive character. She ruled his house, regulated his domestic affairs, and was his chief minister. In all matters within the curtilage, indeed, she was the head. Within this boundary and in all that pertained thereto, with a single exception, she was supreme. That exception was his old desk or "secretary." It was sacred even from her, consecrated to him alone. There were kept piles of old letters, and bundles of old papers in what appeared to her orderly mind a strange confusion; but which he always declared was the perfection of order, though it invariably took him a long time to find any particular paper he might want, a difficulty which he attributed to the occasion when she had once shortly after marriage attempted in his absence to "put things in order." Since then she had regarded the desk and its contents with profound reverence. He repaid her by holding her as the incarnation of all wisdom and virtue. He stood before her as before an inscrutable and superior being. He intrusted to her all his personal affairs, temporal and spiritual. He could not have secured an abler administrator. She was his complement, the unseen influence which made him what he was. She created the atmosphere in which he shone.

His professional life, once begun, went on. The law is an enlistment for life and the battle is ever in array. No client who ever appeared with the requisite certificate of clientage was ever refused. There was no picking and choosing. The old lawyer was a sworn officer of the court, a constituent element of the great juridical system of the country. Whoever wanted legal advice, and applied to him for it, was entitled to it and received it. From that moment the relation of counsel and client began. It was a sacred relation. His clients were his "clients" in the good old original sense of the term. They were not merely persons who came into an office and bought and paid for so much professional service; they were his clients, who confided in his protection as their patron, and received it. The requisite preliminaries, it is true, had to be satisfactorily arranged; the client had to recognize his importance; his authority as his counsel; the good fortune he had in securing his services; he had to promise to transfer to him a proper portion of his personal estate as a proof that he did understand the full measure of this good fortune, and then he became his counsel. From this moment the client had obtained the use of a new force. From this moment he "had counsel." Every power and every resource were devoted to his service. No time was too precious to be spent, no labor too arduous to be endured in his behalf. Body, mind, and soul, his counsel had flung himself into his cause; guided by his professional instinct, spurred by his professional pride, he identified himself with his client's cause, ready to live for it, fight for it, and if necessary even die for it. Public opinion had nothing to do with his undertaking a case. He thought but of his profession. He would, if applied to, defend a client whom if he had not been applied to he would willingly have hung.

Once in a case, he never gave up; if possible he carried it on to success, or if he were defeated he expended every intellectual resource in trying to recover; he was ready to move for new trials, to appeal, to apply for rehearings, and if at the end he were still unsuccessful, he went down damning every one opposed to him, counsel, client, and bench, as a parcel of fools who did not know the law when he put it under their very noses. No wonder that the clients regarded their counsel with veneration!

In a trial he was a new being; his eye brightened; his senses quickened; his nerves thrilled; his form straightened; every power, every force, was called into play; he was no longer a mere lawyer, he was a gladiator in an intellectual contest where the intellect was strung to its highest pitch; a soldier fighting for a cause where reason was wrought in plain, pure, unmistakable nakedness; where every force of the human mind was called into action, and every chord of the human heart was at hand to be played upon.

Before a judge he was powerful; for he argued from the bed-rock principles. This was his strength. He was trained to it. Often retained on the court green just before the case was called at bar, in out-of-the-way places where there were no books, he was forced to rely upon his reason; and his reason and his cause equally prospered. One of his maxims was, "Common law is common sense." Another was, "The reason of the law is the life of the law." He did not need books; as was said, no man had more contempt for authorities, no man had more respect for authority.

But if he was potent before a judge, before a jury he was supreme. For pleading he had little or no respect. It was to be accepted as one of the eccentricities of the profession; it was like some of the unaccountable and inscrutable things in the old dispensation, to be accepted in silence; it was a mystery. His great aim was to come to the jury. He often filed a blank declaration, secure in the knowledge that his opponent would take no advantage of him, knowing that next time he might file a blank declaration himself. The real thing was, in the words of one of them, "to brush way the little chinquapin bush p'ints and get at the guts of the case."

He held men generally in some contempt; but as they approached in the scale to the dignity of members of the bar, his estimation of them rose. The old clerks, as standing in a close relation to the bar, were his friends, stood high in his regard, and were admitted to a share of his intimacy. The bench he treated with all respect, his true feelings for the persons who sat on it being perhaps sometimes veiled, as it was the position not the man that he respected; but his affection, his enthusiasm, were reserved for the bar. The profession of the law was to him the highest of all professions. It was a brotherhood; it was sacred; it maintained the rights of man, preserved the government, controlled the administration of law. It was the profession of Bacon, and Coke, and Clarendon; of Lord Hardwicke and Lord Mansfield; of Pratt and Eldon and Erskine; of Pendleton, Henry, and Wythe, and the greatest of his race and kind. It was the profession which created the liberties of man and preserved the rights of man.

Membership in it was a patent to the possessor, a freemasonry, a tie like that of close common blood which made every member of the bar "a brother lawyer." Every member was assumed to be all right, in virtue of his position, without further question; when one failed and was found wanting, he dropped out. Special terms of reprobation were adopted, such as "Shyster" and "Pettifogger," the full significance of which was known only to the profession. The extreme penalty was disbarring. It was deemed as great a disgrace as any other criminal sentence. Shrewdness might possibly save the malefactor this extreme result; but if he were guilty he was sentenced by the opinion of the bar in its severest term. He was "unprofessional."

These things maintained an exalted standard in the profession. They created a sustaining atmosphere. Wherever the old lawyer went he felt it sensibly. He could not be a lawyer and not be a better and a stronger man. He recognized it; he made others recognize it; it was a controlling motive in his life. He practised on this basis, and as a result he elevated his profession and made it better than he found it.

In conversation he was brilliant. The whole field of law, of literature, history, philosophy, was his domain. In all of them he ranged at will, exhibiting a knowledge, an intelligence, a critical faculty, which were astonishing. Though he never wrote a line, he was a philosopher, a wit, a poet. His knowledge of human nature was profound. It was his chief study. He nearly always spoke of men in the aggregate with contempt; of the times as "degenerate"; yet in actual intercourse his conduct was at variance with his talk; he treated every one with respect. He was in ordinary intercourse serious even to gravity, as one who bore heavy responsibilities; it was only with his particular friends at home, or with his "brothers of the bar" on circuit, that he unbent. His fund of anecdote was inexhaustible. He told stories which kept his companions roaring; told them with inimitable aptness and delicious humor; among them he was a boy, jovial, rollicking; yet, let but a fool approach, and he was dignity itself. To young lawyers he was all kindness. He treated them with a courtesy which was knightly, with a gentleness and consideration which were almost tenderness. In private intercourse he called them by their names, with that flattering familiarity so pleasing to young men. In public he referred to them as "the learned counsel" or "my distinguished young brother." They repaid it by worshipping him.

It was when he discoursed of law that the real power of his intellect was shown. He spoke of it with affection, with reverence, with enthusiasm. Under his analysis the most intricate problems appeared plain, the most eccentric phases resolved themselves into reason, the "common law was common sense." It was not the law as administered by fallible judges in petty courts; it was the law on which Littleton and Coke and Blackstone and Tucker had expended their powers; the law in its roundness, its beauty, its perfection, worthy to have for its seat "the bosom of God," and for its voice "the harmony of Nature."

He was sometimes profane, but never blasphemous; he was not even generally profane, for he regarded speech as a fine instrument to be employed rightly. But on occasion he swore with vehemence, with power, with unction; properly employing his oaths for purposes of superlative malediction.

In his opinions, outside of the law, he was earnest, bigoted, intolerant. His speech was often ferocious; his action was ever the reverse. He was generous to lavishness. He kept open house, and dispensed a boundless hospitality, usually living up to and often beyond his means; if he did not spend his money, some friend for whom he had gone security almost infallibly would. He was frequently in pecuniary embarrassment; yet he was honest. He sometimes even borrowed money from his clients; but it was done in an open way, with their consent, and always without the least idea of not repaying it. The case may be cited of one who, in a suit, being asked what he did with his client's money which he had collected, replied:

"Put it in my bank, sir, to my credit, and drew on it at my own sweet will, as is customary among gentlemen of ample means and greater expectations."

He was more charitable than the rector; no one ever appealed to him for aid in vain; he would lend even if he had to borrow to do it. "His pity gave ere charity began."

He knew every man in his circuit, knew him and his father, and often had known his grandfather before him; knew his history and all his concerns; was privy (not in the legal sense) to his whole life, and to his every act, frequently to the lives of his parents; for his familiarity with the affairs of his section was minute, universal. Perhaps it was not to be wondered at that with this intimate knowledge he held men at large in some contempt. He was not always a professing Christian; often he was not a member of any church; but his wife was, and this made it all right in his eyes. His failure to be a professing Christian was usually caused less by want of piety than by humility, a sense of personal unworthiness; but he did justice, loved mercy, and walked humbly with his God.

His reputation, like his infirmities, increased with his years. Often in his latter days he was forced against his will into political life, where he achieved immediate renown. If he did not enter politics, often he was more potent than if he did. Frequently he was called on in times of great popular fervor or excitement to speak to the people, who relied upon him and wanted his counsel. Generally his eloquence was overwhelming. He made speeches the reputation of which long survived him.

He died poor, leaving no written memorial of his labors; often his very name was in a generation or two forgot. But he was the best missed man in his section. He was missed by all; but most of all by the poor, by the helpless; by widows and orphans. It was only after he passed away that his deeds of kindness were known; that his full worth was recognized. As when a great oak is overthrown by the tempest, its magnitude can be told by the rent it has made, so after he passed from them men came to know how great he had been by the void he left.

Tradition took up his name and handed down stories of his prowess at the bar which lived, though as time passed they were attached to other names, and his was lost. There was recorded no memorial of his work at the bar; but for all that his work survived. He left as the fruit of his labors that which he himself would have deemed the highest reward: large services rendered his fellowmen; much charity done in secret; a good name, and an unsullied profession.

THE OLD-TIME NEGRO

THE OLD-TIME NEGRO

I

THAT the "old-time Negro" is passing away is one of the common sayings all over the South, where once he was as well known as the cotton-plant and the oak tree. Indeed, he has become so rare that even now when a gray and wrinkled survivor is found he is regarded as an exceptional character, and he will soon be as extinct as the dodo. That he will leave a gap which can hardly be filled is as certain as that the old-time cavalier or the foster-father of romance has left his gap.

The "new issue" at which the old-time Negro, who had been the servant and the associate of gentlemen, once turned up his nose from his well-secured position, and of which he spoke in terms of scornful reprobation, has, with the passing of time, pushed him from his stool, and is no longer the "new issue," but the general type that prevails commonly—the Negro with his problem; a problem which it may, as has been well said by Mr. Root, take all the wisdom, all the forbearance, and all the resolution of the white race to solve.

Some of the "Afro-Americans," with the veneer of a so-called education, to judge from recent works written by certain of them, presume to look down somewhat scornfully on this notable development of their race, and assume a fine scorn of the relation which once existed all over the South between the old-time Southerner and the old-time darky, and which still exists where the latter still survives.

They do not consider that large numbers of this class held positions of responsibility and trust, which they discharged with a fidelity and success that is the strongest proof of the potentiality of the race. They do not reckon that warm friendship which existed between master and servant, and which more than any other one thing gives promise of future and abiding friendship between the races when left to settle their relations without outside interference.

One going through the South now—even through those parts where the old-time darky was once the regular and ordinary picture—unless he should happen to drift into some secluded region so far out of the sweep of the current that its life has been caught as in an eddy, would never know what the old life had been, and what the old-time Negroes were in that life. Their memory is still cherished in the hearts of those to whom they stood in a relation which cannot be explained to and cannot be understood by those who did not know it as a vital part of their home-life. Even these will soon have passed from the stage, and in another decade or two the story of that relation, whose roots were struck deep in the sacredest relations of life, will be only a tradition kept alive for a generation or two, but gradually fading until it is quite blurred out by time.

Curiously, whatever the Southerners may think of slavery—and there were many who reprobated its existence—whatever they may think of "the Negro" of to-day, there is scarcely one who knew the Negro in his old relation who does not speak of him with sympathy and think of him with tenderness. The writer has known men begin to discuss new conditions fiercely, and on falling to talking of the past, drift into reminiscences of old servants and turn away to wipe their eyes. And not the least part of the bitterness of the South over the Negro question as it has existed grows out of resentment at the destruction of what was once a relation of warm friendship and tender sympathy.

Of African slavery it may be said that whatever its merits and demerits, it divided this country into two sections, with opposing interests, and finally plunged it into a vast and terrible war. This is condemnation enough.

One need not be an advocate of slavery because he upsets ideas that have no foundation whatever in truth and sets forth facts that can be substantiated by the experience of thousands who knew them at first hand.

II

It is well known by those who knew the old plantation-life that there were marked divisions between the Negroes. There were among them what might almost be termed different orders. These were graded by the various relations in which the individuals stood to the "white folks"

—that is, to the master and mistress and their family.

The house-servants represented a class quite distinct from and quite above the "field-hands," of whom they were wont to speak scornfully as "cornfield niggers," while among the former were degrees as clearly defined as ever existed in an English gentleman's house, where the housekeeper and the butler held themselves above the rest of the servants, only admitting to occasional fellowship the lady's maid.

Among the first in station were the mammy, the butler, the body-servant, the carriage-driver, the ladies' maids, the cook, and the gardener, with, after an interval, the "boys" who were attached to one or the other position as assistants and were in training for the places when the elders should fail. Among the "field-hands" was, first, the "head man."[1]

The "head man" was the equal of any other servant—a rank due, perhaps, partly to his authority and partly to the character that brought him this authority. He was the fore-

[1] The name "driver" was unknown in Virginia, whatever it may have been in the South. And the "driver" of slave-horror novels was as purely the creature of the imagination as Cerberus, or the Chimera.

man, or assistant superintendent of the planta-tion. He carried the keys; he called the hands to work; directed them, and was, to some extent, in authority over them. Such a one I knew, mighty in word and act, who towered above the hands he led, a "head man," indeed.

A somewhat inaccurate idea prevails of the Southern plantation life, due, possibly, to the highly colored pictures that have been painted of it in books of a romantic order, in which the romance much outweighed the ha'penny-worth of verisimilitude. The current idea is that a Southern plantation was generally a great estate, teeming with black slaves who groaned under the lash of the drivers and at night were scourged to their dungeons, while their masters revelled in ill-used luxury and steeped them-selves in licentiousness, not stopping at times to "traffic in their own flesh and blood."

It may be well to say in the outset that nothing could be further from the truth.

There were great estates, but they were not numerous. There were, possibly, a score of per-sons in Virginia who owned over three hundred slaves, and ten or a dozen who owned over five hundred. Such estates were kept up in a certain style which almost always accompanies large

wealth. But the great majority of the plantations in Virginia, and, so far as my reading and
observation have gone, elsewhere, however extensive were the lands, were modest and simple,
and the relation between masters and servants
was one of close personal acquaintance and
friendliness, beginning at the cradle and
scarcely ending at the grave.

At the outbreak of the war, while the number of the white population of the Southern
States was about thirteen millions, the number
of slave-owners and slave-hirers, including those
who owned or hired but one slave, was, perhaps, less than half a million; that is, of the
adult whites, men and women, estimating them
as one-fifth each of the population, less than one
in ten owned or hired slaves.[1]

Thus, while slavery on the great plantations,
where the slaves numbered several hundreds,
was liable to such abuses as spring readily from
absenteeism, on most of the plantations the
slaves and the masters were necessarily brought
into fairly close contact, and the result of this
contact was the relation of friendship which has

[1] In Georgia, for example, as shown by the investigation
of Professor Du Bois, one of the best educated and trained
colored men in the South, there were, in 1860, 455,698
negroes and 591,550 whites. Of these, there were 3,500

been the wonder and the mystification of those who considered slavery the sum of all the villainies.

The chief idea that prevails as to the relation is taken from a work of fiction which, as a political pamphlet written under the stress of deep feeling, whatever truth it had as basis, certainly does not present a true picture.

Work was parcelled out among the "hands," the hands being divided into sections: plough-hands, drivers, hoe-hands, etc.

Their homes were known as "the quarters." On the larger plantations they were divided by streets.

On the plantation which the writer knew best, there were several double-cabins on the quar-

free negroes and 462,195 slaves owned by 40,773 slave-holders, or about 10½ to each slave-holder.

Of these slave-holders,

16 per cent. of all—6,713 owned		1 slave.		
10 " " —4,353 "		2 slaves.		
8 " " —3,482 "		3 "		
	2,984 "	4 "		
	2,543 "	5 "		
	2,213 "	6 "		
	1,839 "	7 "		
	1,647 "	8 "		
	1,415 "	9 "		
	4,707 "	10 or under 15 slaves.		
	2,523 "	15 " " 20 "		
	2,910 "	20 " " 30 "		

ters-hill and three or four facing on the back-
yard. In one of the latter was a room which
was the joy of his heart, and which, after forty
years, is still touched with a light more radiant
than many a palace apartment he has seen. It
was known as "Unc' Balla's room," and its
occupant was so great a man to me that in his
own field I have never known his superior.
"Uncle Balla" was the carriage-driver, and not
from Jehu down was ever one who, in the
writer's mind, could equal him in handling the
reins. He was the guide, philosopher, and
friend of my boyhood. And no better, saner, or
more right-minded guide ever lived.

In that room were "chists," which I even now
think of with an indrawing of the breath, as I
imagine their precious and unexplored contents.

1,400 owned	30 or under	40 slaves
739 "	40 " "	50 "
729 "	50 " "	70 "
373 "	70 " "	100 "
181 "	100 " "	200 "
23 "	200 " "	300 "
7 "	300 " "	500 "
1 "	500 " "	1,000 "

From this table it will be seen that 6,713, or about 16½
per cent., owned only one slave, 10½ per cent. owned only
two slaves, and 50 per cent. owned five slaves or fewer, while
66 per cent. (27,191) owned under ten slaves; 1,102 owned
between fifty and one hundred, and but 212 owned over one
hundred, while only twenty-three owned over two hundred.

Verily, they must have held golden ingots! Then, there was his cobbler's bench, for he was a harness-maker and cobbler—and his cooper's bench, for he made the noggins and piggins and pails for the milkmaids and housewives, deriving therefrom a little income. And when it came to horses! As I have sat and heard the learned at races and horse-shows air their knowledge, I have often been filled with a sudden longing that Uncle Balla were there to show what real knowledge was.

He lived for thirty years after the war in a little house on the edge of the plantation, and when he began to fail he was brought home, where he could be better looked after. At the end, his funeral services were conducted from the front portico and he was followed to the grave by white and black.

Each cabin had, or might have had, its little yard and garden, and each family had its chicken-house and yard.

On the larger plantations, where the Negroes numbered two hundred or more, nearly everything was made by them, so that such an estate was a little world in itself, substantially self-supporting. On our place, while the spinning and weaving and the carpentry-work were done on the place, most of the cloth for clothing and the shoes were bought in town in the spring and autumn, and the tailor and cobbler kept them in order. In purchasing the shoes, each person brought his measure, a stick the exact length of his foot. This stick had certain marks or notches on it, and the Negro kept a duplicate, by which to identify his shoes when they arrived.

III

No servants or retainers of any race ever identified themselves more fully with their masters. The relation was rather that of retainers than of slaves. It began in the infancy of both master and servant, grew with their growth, and continued through life. Such a relation does not now, so far as I know, exist, except in the isolated instances of old families who have survived all the chances and changes with the old family servants still hanging on. Certainly, I think, it did not exist anywhere else, unless, perhaps, on the country estates of the gentry in England and, possibly, in parts of France and Germany.

311

This relation in the South was not exceptional. It was the general, if not the universal rule. The servants were "my servants" or "my people"; the masters were to the servants, "*my* master and *my* mistis," or "my white folks." Both pride and affection spoke in that claim.

In fact, the ties of pride were such that it was often remarked that the affection of the slaves was stronger toward the whites than toward their own offspring. This fact, which cannot be successfully disputed, has been referred by Professor Shaler to a survival of a tribal instinct which preponderated over the family instinct. Others may possibly refer it to the fact that the family instinct was, owing to the very nature of the institution of slavery, not allowed to take deep root. Whatever the cause, it does not appear even now to have taken much root, at least, according to the standard of the Anglo-Saxon, a race whose history is founded upon the family instinct.

The family ties among the Negroes often appear to be scarcely as strong now as they were under the institution of slavery. Marital fidelity is, if we are to believe those who have had good opportunities of observation, not as common now as it was then. The instances of desertion of husbands, of wives, of parents, or children would possibly offset any division that took place under that institution.

A number of old Negroes whom I have known have been abandoned by nearly all of their children. Often, when they grow up, they leave them with scarcely less unconcern than do any order of the lower animals.

The oldest son of our dining-room servant went off at the time of one of Sheridan's raids and was never heard of again until some twenty years after the war, when it was learned that he was a fisherman on the lower James, and although he lived, and may be living yet, within a hundred miles of his old home, where his father and mother lived, he never took the trouble even to communicate with them once. The next son went off to the South after the war, and the only time that he ever wrote home, so far as I know, was when he wrote to ascertain his age, in order that he might qualify to vote. The same may be said of many others.

The Mammy was, perhaps, the most important of the servants, as she was also the closest intimate of the family. She was, indeed, an actual member of the household. She was usually selected in her youth to be the companion of the children by reason of her being the child of some favored servant and, as such, likely to possess sense, amiability, judgment, and the qualities which gave promise of character and efficiency. So she grew up in intercourse with the girls of the family, and when they married she became, in turn, the nurse and assistant to the old mammy, and then the mammy of her young mistress's children, and, after, of their children. She has never been adequately described. Chiefly, I fancy, because it was impossible to describe her as she was.

Who may picture a mother? We may dab and dab at it, but when we have done our best we know that we have stuck on a little paint, and the eternal verity stands forth like the eternal verity of the Holy Mother, outside our conception, only to be apprehended in our highest moments, and never to be truly pictured by pen or pencil.

So, no one can describe what the Mammy was, and only those can apprehend her who were rocked on her generous bosom, slept on her bed, fed at her table, were directed and controlled by her, watched by her unsleeping eye, and led by her precept in the way of truth, justice, and humanity.

She was far more than a servant. She was a member of the family in high standing and of unquestioned influence. She was her mistress's coadjutress and her wise adviser, and where the children were concerned, she was next to her in authority.

My father's mammy, old Krenda, was said to have been an African princess, and whether there was any other foundation for the idea than her commanding presence and character, I know not; but these were unquestionable. Her aphorisms have been handed down in the family since her time. Among them was one which has a smack of the old times and at least indicates that she had not visited some modern cities: "Good manners will cyah you whar money won't."

I remember my mammy well, though she died when I was a child. Her name was Lydia, and she was the daughter of old Betty, who had been my great-grandmother's maid. Betty used to read to her mistress during the latter years of her life when she was blind. Lydia had been my mother's mammy before she was mine and my brother's, and she had the authority and prestige of having been such.

After forty-five years, I recall with mingled

affection and awe my mammy's dignity, force, and kindness; her snowy bed, where I was put to sleep in the little up-stairs room, sealed with pictures from the illustrated papers and with fashion-plates, in which her artistic feeling found its vent; I recall also the delicious "biscuit-bread" she made, which we thought better than that of all the cooks and bakers in the world. In one corner stood her tea-table, with her "tea-things," her tea and white sugar.

I remember, too, the exercise of her authority, and recall at least two "good whippings" that she gave me.

One curious recollection that remains is of a discussion between her and one of her young mistresses on the subject of slavery, in which the latter fell back on what is, possibly, one of the strongest arguments of the slave-holder, the Bible, and asserted that God had put each of them in their places. It may be left to the reader to say which had the better of the argument. The interest of the matter now is rather academic than practical.

A few days before my mammy's death she made her will, dividing her "things," for such wills were as strictly observed as if they had been admitted to probate. Among her bequests her feather-bed and pillows were left to my elder brother. She made my mother bring a pen and write his name on the bed and pillows. And these pillows are now in his rectory.

It was from our mammies that we learned those delightful stories of "Brer Fox" and "Brer Hyah," which the children of a later generation have learned through the magic pen of "Uncle Remus." It was from them also that we learned many of the lessons of morality and truth.

Next to the mammy in point of dignity was, of right, the butler. He held much the same position that is held by the butler in English houses. He was a person in authority, and he looked that every inch. He had his ideas, and they usually prevailed. He was the governor of the young children, the mentor of the young men, and their counsellor even after they had grown up.

Some of my readers may have seen in some hotel a Negro head-waiter who was a model of dignity and of grave authority—a field-marshal in ebony—doing the honors of his dining-room like a court chamberlain, and ruling his subordinates with the authority of a benignant despot. Such a one was probably some gentleman's butler, who had risen by his abilities to be the chief of the dining-room.

More than one such character rises before me from the past, and the stories of their authority are a part of the traditional record of every family. The most imposing one that I personally remember was "Uncle Tom," the butler of a cousin, whose stateliness impressed my childhood's fancy in a way which has never been effaced. I have seen monarchs less impressive. His authority was so well recognized that he used to be called in to make the children take their physic.

It was said that one of the children, who is now a matron of great dignity and a grandmother, once, in an awed whisper, asked her grandmother, who was the mistress of "Uncle Tom" and of several hundred other servants, "Gran'ma, is you feared o' Unc' Tom?" And her grandmother, who told the story, used to add: "And you know the truth is, I am."

It was a cousin of hers, Mrs. Carter, of Shirley, who used to say that when she invited company she always had to break it to Clarissy, her maid.

In truth, whatever limitation there was on the unstinted hospitality of the South was due to the fact that the servants were always considered in such matters.

This awe of the butler in his grandeur often did not pass away with youth. He both demanded and received his due respect even from grown members of the family. Of one that I knew it is told now by gray-headed men how, on occasion, long after they were grown, he would correct their manners, even at table, by a little rap on the head and a whispered reproof, as he leaned over them to place a dish. And I never knew one who did not retain his position of influence and exercise his right of admonition.

I have known butlers to take upon themselves the responsibility of saying what young gentlemen should be admitted as visitors at the house, and to whom the ladies should be denied. In fact, every wise young man used to be at pains to make friends with the old servants, for they were a sagacious class and their influence in the household was not inconsiderable. They had an intuitive knowledge, which amounted to an instinct, for "winnowing the grain from the chaff," and they knew a "gent'man" at sight. Their acute and caustic comments have wrecked the chances of many an aspiring young suitor who failed to meet with their approval.

IV

THERE is a universal belief that the Negroes under slavery had no education. I have seen it stated a number of times that it was made a crime by law, in every State of the South, to teach one to read. Such a statement is not true.[1] Teaching them was not encouraged, generally, and such laws existed at one time in four of the States of the South; but they did not exist in Virginia. Several of our Negroes could read, and if it was not the same on most of the plantations, it was at least the same on those of which I had any knowledge. My great-grandmother's maid used, I have heard, to read to her regularly, and in our family the ladies used to teach the girls as much as they would

[1] As to the education of the Negroes: See Report of U. S. Commissioner of Education, 1901, vol. i, p. 745, *et seq.*, for a valuable paper by Prof. Kelly Miller, one of the most intelligent colored men in the country. Citing the Report of U. S. Commissioner of Education, 1868, he shows that such laws were adopted in Alabama, Georgia, Louisiana, and South Carolina, about 1830-34. While in Virginia in 1831, as in Delaware in 1886, all public meetings were prohibited. These laws grew out of the Nat Turner Insurrection. V. Appendix.

learn. But apart from book-learning, they had, especially the house-servants, the education which comes from daily association with people of culture, and it was an education not to be despised. Some gentlemen carried on a correspondence about home affairs with their butlers during their absence from home. For instance, I recall hearing that when Mr. Abel P. Upshur was Secretary of the Navy, some gentlemen were at his house, and were discussing at table some public matter, when the butler gave them the latest news about it, saying that he had that morning received a letter from his master.

There is an idea that the Negroes were in the state of excitement and agonized expectancy of freedom that the Anglo-Saxon race felt it would have been in under similar circumstances. Much is made, at certain kinds of meetings, of the great part which they contributed toward saving the Union. Discussion of this may be set aside as bordering on the controversial. But it may not be outside of this phase of the matter, and it will throw some light on it to state briefly what was the attitude of the Negro slave population toward the quarrel between the North and the South.

The total number of Negro enlistments and reënlistments on the Federal side was between 189,000 and 190,000. When it is considered that this embraced all the soldier element of the Negroes in the North and of the refugee element in the South, who were induced to enter the army, either by persuasion of bounties or under stress of compulsion, whether of military draft or of "belly-pinching," the number does not appear large. After midsummer, 1863, the North occupied the States of Maryland, Missouri, Kentucky, half of Virginia, of Tennessee, of Louisiana, of Arkansas, of Mississippi, and considerable portions of the Carolinas and Alabamas. That is, she occupied a third, and nearer a half, of the entire slave-holding territory of the South, while the penetration of her raiding parties into the regions occupied by the Southern troops furnished, at times, opportunity to, possibly, a fourth of the young men of that section to escape from bondage had they been moved by the passion of freedom. It is at once a refutation of the charge of the cruelty of slavery, so commonly accepted, and an evidence of the easy-going amiability and docility of the Negro race that, under all the excitement and through all the opportunities

THE OLD-TIME NEGRO

and temptations surrounding them, they should not only have remained faithful to their masters, but that the stress of the time should have appeared to weld the bond between them.

That there was a wild and adventurous element among them is well known. It was to be expected, and was an element in whom the instincts of wild life in the jungle and the forests survived. Every large plantation had one or more who had the runaway spirit keenly alive. There were several on our place. They ran away when they were crossed in love or in any other desire of their hearts. They ran away if they were whipped, and, as they were the shirkers and loafers on the plantations, if anyone was whipped, it was likely to be one of them. Yet, curiously enough, if a runaway was caught and was whipped, he was very unlikely to run off again until the spirit seized him, when nothing on earth could stop him.[1]

One other class was likely to furnish the ele-

[1] We had three or four such young men on our plantation, and although the plantation lay within two or three miles of the roads down which Sheridan and Stoneman passed, and within twelve or fifteen miles of those along which Grant passed, these were the only negroes from our place who went off during the war. In all four young men left us.

If anyone wishes to get an insight into this phase of the negro character and at the same time pass a delightful half

323

ment that went off, and this was the "pampered class." House-servants were more likely to go than field-hands. Their ears were somehow more attuned to the song of the siren.[1]

Against those who availed themselves of the opportunities offered them to escape from the bondage of domestic slavery may be put the great body of the Negro race who, whether from inability to grasp the vastness of the boon of liberty held out to them, or from fear of the ills they knew not of, or from sheer content with a life where the toil was not drudgery and the fleshpots overbalanced the idea of freedom, not only held fast to their masters, but took sides with them with a quickened feeling and a deepened affection. For every one who fled to freedom, possibly one hundred stood by their masters' wives and children.

Doubtless there were many—possibly, the most of them—who remained from sheer inertia or fear to leave. But a far larger number identified themselves with their masters, and this union was not one of lip-service, but of sentiment, of heart and soul.

hour, let him read Harry Stillwell Edwards's story, "Two Runaways."

[1] That very "Uncle Tom," of whom I have spoken as a stern and terrifying spectacle of grandeur, left his home and went to Philadelphia.

In truth, they were infected with the same spirit and ardor that filled the whites, and had the South called for volunteers from the Negroes, I question not that they could have gotten half a million men. [1]

A story is told of one of the old Negroes who belonged to the family into which General Scott married. He went to the war to take care of one of his young masters. He had no doubt whatever as to the justice of the cause, but General Scott was to his mind the embodiment of war and carnage, and the General had espoused the other side. This disturbed him greatly, and one night he was heard praying down outside the camp. After praying for everyone, he prayed: ''And O Lord, please to convut Marse Lieutenan' Gen'l Scott and turn him f'om de urrer o' he ways.''

The devotion of slaves to their masters in time of war is no new thing under the sun. The fact that their masters are in arms has always, no doubt, borne its part in the phenomenon. But it does not wholly account for the absolute devotion of the Negroes. It is to the eternal credit at once of the Whites and of the Negroes that, during these four years of war, when the

[1]Several regiments were enlisted in the beginning of the war, but the plan was changed and they were disbanded.

white men of the South were absent in the field they could intrust their homes, their wives, their children, all they possessed, to the guardianship and care of their slaves, with absolute confidence in their fidelity. And this trust was never violated. The Negroes were their faithful guardians, their sympathizing friends, and their shrewd advisers, guarding their property, enduring necessary denial with cheerfulness, and identifying themselves with their masters' fortunes with the devotion, not of slaves, but of clansmen.

The devotion of the body-servants to their masters in the field is too well known almost to need mention, and what is said of them in this paper is owing rather to the feeling that the statement of the fact is a debt due to the class from which these came rather than to thinking it necessary to enlighten the reader.

When the Southern men went into the field there was always a contest among the Negroes as to who should accompany them. Usually, the choice of the young men would be for some of the younger men among the servants, while the choice of the family would be for some of the older and more staid members of the household, who would be prudent, and so, more likely to take better care of their masters. And thus there was much heart-burning among the younger Negroes, who were almost as eager for adventure as their masters.

Of all the thousands of Negroes who went out as servants with their masters, I have never heard of one who deserted to the North, and I have known of many who had abundant opportunity to do so. Some were captured, but escaped; others apparently deserted, but returned laden with spoils.

My fathers body-servant, Ralph Woodson, served with him throughout the entire war. While at Petersburg, where the armies were within a mile of each other, he was punished for getting drunk and he ran away. But instead of making for the Union lines and surrendering to a Union picket, which he could easily have done, he started for home, sixty miles away. He was, however, arrested as a straggler or runaway, and my father, hearing of him, sent and brought him back to camp, where he remained to the end.

An even more notable instance which has come to my knowledge was that of Simon, the servant of a friend of mine. He disappeared from camp during the Spottsylvania campaign, and just when his master had given him up he reappeared with a sack full of all sorts of things, useful for the mess, which he declared "dem gent'mens on the other side had gin him." He had borrowed of the Egyptians.

The letters and annals of the time are full of reference to the singular, but then well-known fact, that while the people of the South gave their sons joyfully to the cause, they were most unwilling to allow their Negroes to go. The reason for this has been much misapprehended. It has been generally supposed outside that it was because they were afraid to lose their property. Nothing could be more unfounded. They were afraid their servants might be hurt or suffer some harm.

Fathers who wrote their sons to be always at the post of honor, would give them explicit directions how to keep their servants out of danger. The war in some way was concerned with the perpetuation of slavery, and it was felt that it was not just to expose slaves to danger when such was the case.

Something of this same feeling played its part in the decision not to enlist Negroes in the army of the Confederacy.

In the field they showed both courage and

sagacity, and many are the instances in which, when their masters were wounded and left on the field, they hunted for them through scenes which tested men's courage as much as the battle itself. The records of the time are full of such instances.

V

When the war closed and the Negroes were set free, the feeling between them and their old masters was never warmer, the bonds of friend-ship were never more close. The devotion which the Negro had shown during the long struggle had created a profound impression on the minds of the Southern whites. Even be-tween the Negroes and poorer whites, who had always been rather at enmity, a better feeling had grown up. The close of the war had ac-complished what all the emancipation procla-mations could not effect. Their masters uni-versally informed their servants that they were free.

I remember my father's return from Appo-mattox. For days he had been watched for. Appomattox was less than a hundred miles from our home. The news of the surrender had come to us first through one of the wagon-drivers, who told it weeping. I seem to see the return now—my father on his gray horse, with his body-servant, Ralph, behind him. I remember the way in which, as he slipped from his horse, he put his hand over his face to hide his tears, and his groan, "I never expected to come home so." All were weeping. A few minutes later he came out on the porch and said: "Ralph, you are free; take the saddles off and turn the horses out."

He had carried a silver half-dollar all through the war, saving it till the last pinch. This had come when he reached the river on his way home. The ferryman had declined to take Confederate money, and he paid him his half-dollar to ferry him across.

Such was the end of slavery, the institution which had divided this country in twain, and finally had convulsed it and brought on a terrible war.

When the end of slavery came there was, doubtless, some heart-burning, but the transition was accomplished without an outbreak, and well-nigh without one act of harshness or even of rudeness.

If there was jubilation among the Negroes on the plantation it was not known to the Whites. In fact the Negroes were rather mystified. The sudden coming of that for which they had possibly hoped, with the loom of the unknown future, had sobered at least the elders. Their owners, almost without exception, conveyed to them the information of their freedom, which thus had a more comprehensible security than could have been given by the acts of Congress, or the orders of military authorities.

In some cases the old Negroes sought and held long conferences with their mistresses or masters in which the whole matter was canvassed.

In every instance the assurance was given them that they should live on the old plantations, if they wished to do so and were still willing to work and would obey orders.

As was natural, the Negroes, in the first flush of freedom, left the estates and went off ''for themselves,'' as the phrase ran.[1] They flocked either to the cities, or to the nearest centre where a garrison of Union troops was posted,

[1] Prince Kropotkin mentioned in his memoirs that the Russian serfs who wanted to show their emancipation did the same thing.

and where rations were distributed partly as a measure of necessity and partly from a philanthropic sentiment which had more or less ground for its existence. But after a time, many of them returned to work. Those of them who had anything shared what they had with their masters. Some of them brought eggs and chickens; others saved a part of the rations given by the Government.

It is no part of my intention in this paper to go generally into the relation of the two races since the emancipation of the Negroes. Certain phases of this relation have been dealt with by me elsewhere. While it is easy to see what mistakes have been made in dealing with the subject, no one can tell with any assurance how a different system might have worked out. All we can say, with absolute certainty, is that hardly any other system could have been more disastrous than the one which was adopted.

One fact, I think, cannot be soundly controverted—that the estrangement of the Negro from the white race in the South is the greatest misfortune that has befallen the former in his history, not excepting his ravishment from his native land.

VI

THE old-time Negro has almost quite passed from the earth, as have his old master and his old mistress. A few still remain, like the last leaves on the tree, but in no long time they, too, will have disappeared. But so long as he survives, the old family feeling of affection will remain in the hearts of those who knew him. Every week or two the newspapers contain the mention of the passing from the stage of one or more of those whose place in some old family made them notable in their lives and caused them to be followed to the grave by as sincere mourners among the whites as among the blacks. But how many of them pass without any other notice than the unfeigned mourning of those whom they loved and served so faithfully!

No Southerner, whatever his feelings of antagonism may be to the Negro race, ever meets an old Negro man or woman without that feeling rising in his breast which one experiences when he meets some old friend of his youth on whom Time has laid his chastening hand.

Nor has the old feeling by any means died out in the breast of the old Negro himself. Only as the whites look on the young blacks with some disapproval, so the old Negro regards the younger generation of whites as inferior to the generation he knew.

Not long since a friend in Richmond told me the following story: A friend of his in that city invited him in the shooting season to go down to his father's place to shoot partridges. The house had been burned down, but old Robin was still living there, and had told him not long before that there were a good many birds on the place. Accordingly, the two gentlemen one morning took their guns and dogs and drove down to the old Ball plantation, where they arrived about sunrise. Old Robin was cutting wood in front of his cabin, and my friend began to shout for him: "Oh, Robin! Oh, Robin!" The old fellow stopped, and coming to the brow of the hill above them, called: "Who dat know me so much bettuh den I know him?"

"Come down here!" called his master.

When the old fellow discovered who it was he was delighted.

"Yes, suh," said he; "dyah 's plenty of buds

334

down here on de branch. I sees 'em eve'y evenin' most when I comes down atter my cow. You go 'long and kill 'em and I 'll take keer of yo' horse for yo' and tell Mandy to hev some snack for yo' 'bout twelve o'clock.''

Just as he was leaving, he stopped, and leaning out of the wagon, said: ''Marse Gus, don't yo' shoot any ole hyahs down here. I takes my gun down wid me when I goes down atter my cow. Dem buds flies too fas' for me, but I kin manage to shoot a ole hyah if I ketch one settin' in the baid.''

The promise was given and was kept by the hunters until they were about to stop for lunch. Just then a fine hare jumped up in front of Marse Gus, and gave him a fair shot. In his ardor he fired at it and knocked it over. At that moment old Robin was heard calling to them to come on up to the house as ''snack was ready.''

''There!'' said Gus, as he picked up the hare, ''now I 've gone and killed this hare, and that old man will never forgive me.''

''Take it and give it to him for his wife,'' said his friend.

''Oh, no!'' he said, ''you don't know old Robin; he will never forgive me.''

335

"Well, put it down in the bottom of your game-bag; he will never know the difference," said his friend. And this was shamelessly done.

They were greeted by the old man cheerfully, with "You must have got plenty of buds, I heard you shoot so much?"

"Oh, yes, we had very good luck!" said the huntsmen.

"You did n't shoot any ole hyahs?" he inquired confidently.

The silence aroused his suspicion, and, turning, he shot a keen glance at his master, which took in the well-filled game-bag.

"What you got in dem game-pockets to make 'em look so big? You certain'y ain' shoot as many buds as dat in dis time?"

Gus, convicted, poked his hand into his bag and drew out the rabbit.

"Here, Uncle Robin," he said in some confusion, "this is the only one I shot. I want you to take it and give it to Mandy."

But the old man declined. "Nor, I don't want it and Mandy don' want it," he said, half-scornfully; "you done shoot it and now yo' better keep it."

He stalked on up the hill in silence. Suddenly, stopping, he turned back.

"Well, well," he said, "times certain'y is changed! Marse Gus, yo' pa would n't 'a' told me a lie for a mule, let 'lone a' ole hyah."

The character of the old-time Negro can hardly be better illustrated than by the case of an old friend of mine, John Dabney, to whom I, in common with nearly all my acquaintances in Richmond, used to be greatly indebted, for he was the best caterer I ever knew. John Dabney was, in his boyhood, a race-rider for a noted Virginia turfman, Major William R. Johnson, but, possibly because of his gifts as a cook, he soon grew too fat for that "lean and hungry" calling, and in time he became a celebrated cook and caterer. He belonged to a lady in the adjoining county to my native county, and, prior to the war, he bought himself from his mistress, as was not infrequently done by clever Negroes. When the war closed, he still owed his mistress several hundred dollars on account of this debt, and as soon as he was able to raise the sum he sent it to her. She promptly returned it, telling him that he was free and would have been free anyhow and that he owed her nothing. On this, John Dabney took the money, went to his old home and insisted on her receiving it, saying that his old master had brought him up to pay his debts, and that this was a just debt which he proposed to pay. And pay it he did.

The instances are not rare in which old family servants who have worked under the new conditions more successfully than their former owners, have shown the old feeling by rendering them such acts of kindness as could only have sprung from a deep and abiding affection.

Whoever goes to the White House will find at the door of the executive offices an elderly and very stout Negro door-keeper, with perfect manners, a step as soft as the fall of the leaf, and an aplomb which nothing can disturb. His name is Arthur Simmons, and, until toward the close of the war, he was a gentleman's servant in North Carolina; then he came North. He is, possibly, the oldest employee in the White House, having been appointed by General Grant during his first term, and having held his position, with the exception of a single term —that of General Harrison—to the present time. It is said that Mr. Cleveland's first appointment after his return to office was that of Arthur Simmons to his old post. Possibly, Mr. Cleveland had heard this story of him: Once, Arthur, having learned that his old mistress had expressed a desire to see the President of the United States, invited her to Washington, met her at the station, saw to her comfort while in the city, arranged an interview with the President for her, and then escorted her back to take her train home.

On a part of the old plantation which I have attempted to describe has lived for the past thirty years, free of rent, the leading Negro politician in the upper end of Hanover County. His wife, Hannah, was my mother's old maid, who, after the war, as before it, served us with a fidelity and zeal of which I can give no conception. It may, however, illustrate it to state that, although she lived a mile and a quarter from the house and had to cross a creek, through which, in times of high water, she occasionally had to wade almost to her waist, she for thirty years did not miss being at her post in the morning more than a half-score times.

Hannah has gone to her long home, and it may throw some light on the old relation between mistress and servant to say that on the occasion of the golden wedding of her old master and mistress, as Hannah was at that time too ill to leave her home, they took all the presents in the carriage and carried them over to

339

show them to her. Indeed, Hannah's last thought was of her old mistress. She died suddenly one morning, and just before her death she said to her husband, "Open the do', it 's Miss——." The door was opened, but the mistress was not there, except to Hannah's dying gaze. To her, she was standing by her bedside, and her last words were addressed to her.

It is a continual cause of surprise among those who do not know the South intimately that Southerners should be so fond of the old Negroes and yet should be so intolerant of things which Northerners would regard with indifference. It is a matter which can hardly be explained, but if anyone goes and lives at the South, he will quickly find himself falling into Southern ways. Let one go on the plantations where the politician is absent and the "bloody-shirt" newspaper is unknown, and he will find something of the old relation still existing.

I have seen a young man (who happened to be a lieutenant in a volunteer company) kiss his old mammy on the parade ground in sight of the whole regiment.

Some years ago, while General Fitzhugh Lee was Governor of Virginia, a wedding took place in the executive mansion at Richmond. At the last moment, when the company were assembled and all had taken their places, waiting for the bride to appear, it was discovered that Mammy Celia, the bride's mammy, had not come in, and no less a person than General Lee, the Governor of Virginia, went and fetched her in on his arm to take her place beside the mother of the bride.

VII

UNHAPPILY, whatever the future may produce, the teachings of doctrinaires and injudicious friends have lost the Negroes of the present generation their manners and cost them much of the friendship of the Whites.

None of us knows what relation the future may produce between the two races in the South, but possibly when the self-righteous shall be fewer than they are now and the teachings which have estranged the races shall become more sane, the great Anglo-Saxon race, which is dominant, and the Negro race, which is amiable, if not subservient, will adjust their differences more in accordance with the laws which must eventually prevail, and the old feeling of kindliness, which seems, under the stress of antagonism, to be dying away, will once more reassert itself.

THE WANT OF A HISTORY OF
THE SOUTHERN PEOPLE

THE WANT OF A HISTORY
OF THE SOUTHERN
PEOPLE

DO we know the true history of the South?
I confess that I do not, nor do I know
where it may be learned.

When Phaon, the Sophist, consulted the oracle, he was directed to inquire of the dead.

"How may this be?" said the people, "seeing that the dead cannot speak?"

The philosopher turned to the records of
their wisdom, and there found the answer he
sought.

If the South to-day should consult the oracle
and receive this answer, whither should she
turn?

The eloquence which once reverberated from
one end of the earth to the other is now an echo;
and the wisdom which created a nation is now

345

the property of every beggar who dares to assert a claim.

There is no true history of the South. In a few years there will be no South to demand a history. What of our history is known by the world to-day? What is our position in history? How are we regarded? Nothing or next to nothing is known of our true history by the world at large. By a limited class in England there is a vague belief founded on a sentiment that the South was the aristocratic section of this country, and that it stood for its rights, even with an indefensible cause. By a somewhat more extended class its heroism is admired sufficiently to partly condone its heresies. But these are a small part of the public. By the world at large we are held to have been an ignorant, illiterate, cruel, semi-barbarous section of the American people, sunk in brutality and vice, who have contributed nothing to the advancement of mankind: a race of slave-drivers, who, to perpetuate human slavery, conspired to destroy the Union, and plunged the country into war. Of this war, precipitated by ourselves, two salient facts are known—that in it we were whipped, and that we treated our prisoners with barbarity. Libby Prison and

Andersonville have become by-words which fill the world with horror. Why should this be, when the real fact is that Libby was the best lighted and ventilated prison on either side; when the horrors of Andersonville were greatly due to the terrible refusal of the Northern government to exchange prisoners or to send medicines to their sick; when the prisoners there fared as well as our men in the field and when the treatment of Southern prisoners in Northern prisons was as bad if not worse and the rate of mortality was as great there as in ours?

We are paraded as still exhibiting unconquered the same qualities untempered by misfortune; as nullifying the Constitution, falsifying the ballot, trampling down a weaker race in an extravagance of cruelty, and with shameless arrogance imperilling the nation as much now as when we went to war.

This is concisely what the outer world thinks of us, and, in the main, honestly thinks of us. As the issues stand and with the record as it is at present made up, this is what posterity will think of us.

The Encyclopædia Britanica is generally deemed a standard authority. It may be assumed to be impartial on all American matters as any other authority. In its article on "American Literature," Vol. 1, p. 719, it says this of the South: "The attractive culture of the South has been limited in extent and degree. The hothouse fruit of wealth and leisure, it has never struck its roots deeply into native soil. Since the Revolution days when Virginia was the nurse of statesmen, the few thinkers of America, born south of Mason and Dixon's line, outnumbered by those belonging to the single State of Massachusetts, have commonly emigrated to New York or Boston in search of a university training. In the world of letters, at least, the Southern States have shone by reflected light; nor is it too much to say that mainly by their connection with the North the Carolinas have been saved from sinking to the level of Mexico or the Antilles."

Think of this! this said of the section that largely has made America, governed her, administered justice from her highest tribunal, commanded her armies and navies, doubled her territory, created her greatness.

How many are here in this audience who cannot tell the name of the ship that brought the Pilgrim Fathers to New England, and then went, according to tradition, on a less paternal pilgrimage? Probably not one!

Now how many are there who can tell the names of the vessels that brought first to the shores of the South the Anglo-Saxon race which reclaimed America, and made it forever the home of liberty and Christianity?

They were the *Discovery*, the *Good-Speed*, and the *Susan-Constant*.

Does not the relative notoriety of the two prove that the history of the South has been regarded with indifference? The men borne hither by these three vessels, and not the passengers on the *Mayflower*, were the Argonauts who first took the Golden Fleece, this golden land.

From that day to this the South has been content to act, and has not cared for the judgment of her contemporaries, much less of posterity. From that day the deeds which have added a new continent to Christendom and have perpetuated the spirit of liberty have been left without other memorial than their own existence to the all-engulfing maw of time.

A people has lived, and after having crowded into two centuries and a half a mightiness of force, a vastness of results, which would have enriched a thousand years, has passed away, and has left no written record of its life. A civilization has existed more unique than any

349

other since the dawn of history, as potent in its influence, and yet no chronicle of it has been made by any but the hand of hostility.

Is there any history of this country which you can place in your boy's hands and say, "This is the true history of your native land?"

I do not belittle the local chroniclers who have preserved from absolute oblivion the records of their native States. On the contrary, I hold them and their unrequited toil in all honor. Except for their labors of love the story of the Old South would have been lost in the abyss of the irreclaimable past; we should have been forced to say as we used to say in the old games of our childhood, "Rats have eaten it and fire has burnt it."

The very records of the country by which our rights of citizenship are established have been lost by reason of this national negligence.

The muniments of title to the property we hold, nay, the very proof of our identity and position, social and legal, have been disregarded and destroyed.

I doubt if a large proportion of the respectable people in the South would not, if they were called on to establish the legal marriage of their grandparents, find themselves compelled to rely on general reputation.

The universal indifference at the South to the preservation of public records is appalling.

It is almost incredible that a race so proud of its position, so assertive of its rights, so jealous of its reputation, should have been so indifferent to all transmission of their memorial.

The solution of the mystery is to be found, I think, in the wonderful rapidity of the development of the country. The progress of the nation was so marvellous that there was no time to record it. Action was so intense and so absorbing that no leisure was found to give to its contemplation. The race was so momentous that young Atalanta had no time to pause even to secure the apples of the Hesperides.

When the stern exactions of colonial life gave place to the gentler phase which advancing civilization brought, the transition was so great and so sudden that the senses were lulled in a sweet oblivion to the demands of the future, and were satisfied with enjoyment of the present. It was a life which the outer world misunderstood and misjudged. The spirit of the Southerner, accustomed as he was to domination, was not such as to take misjudgment meekly. He met it with a pride which success did not temper and defeat could not quell.

He was eminently self-contained, and his own

self-respect satisfied, he cared not for the world's applause. He was content to live according to his own will, and as there was no human tribunal to which he wished to submit his acts, why should he keep a record of his life?

Thus it is, that the only history of the South is that contained in the journals of the time, and in the fragmentary minutes of the polemic warfare in which a large part of the population was unceasingly engaged, and the South is to-day practically without a written history. I cannot accept as her true history the dissertations composed in part of the disjointed records divorced from the circumstances which called them into being, and for the rest, of the lubrications of the hostile or the unsympathetic commentator. Her history must have another source than this.

From the birth of the American people the two sections of the country were the North and the South. Mason and Dixon's line stretched from the East to the West before it received its baptismal name.

The origins of the two populations were different. The tendencies were yet more diverse. Two essentially diverse civilizations were the result. That of the North was compact, cohesive, and commercial. The settlement was in towns or townships. The municipality possessed and exercised powers which never could have been tolerated at the South. That of the South was diffusive and agricultural. It tended to the development of the individual, and to guardfulness of his rights. Assertion of the rights, privileges, and franchises of the individual was the cardinal doctrine of the South. The Southerner bore this with him as an inalienable heritage wherever he went, into primeval forests and across mountain ranges. Kentucky had yet hard work to hold her own against the savage when she was adopting her celebrated resolutions.

The New Englander went to his meetinghouse to receive instruction and to accept direction from the authorized powers, spiritual and temporal.

The Southerner rode through trackless forests to argue questions as to their powers and their authority.

At first the interests of the two sections were not merely not identical, but were conflicting, until the coalition between the French and the Indian, bringing identity of danger, created identity of interest. The tyranny of the British crown continued this cause and brought the two sections, for the purpose of common defence, into a close confederation. The restrictions and the impotency of this confederacy were so great, and the advantages of a "more perfect union" were so manifest, that the Articles of Confederation gave way to a new compact, embracing such "alterations and provisions" as seemed necessary to "render the Federal Constitution adequate to the exigencies of government and the preservation of the Union."

The result was the Constitution of the United States.

Hardly had the Union been established before the divergent interests of the two sections reasserted themselves. From this time the struggle on the part of each was to obtain ascendency, and to control the government, each jealously opposing every attempt on the part of the other to extend its power. Unfortunately, a factor remained which rendered harmony impossible. African slavery, which at one time had been as acceptable at the North as at the South, had been found not suited to the latitude nor to the peculiar civilization which existed there. It was, therefore, in pro-

cess of abolition, and in a comparatively brief
period, through the instrumentalities of emancipation, and of transference, it disappeared at
the North.

After a time hostility to this institution became the excitant of the popular mind against
the South, and 'was the lever with which the
politicians worked the overthrow of this section. At the period of which I speak, however,
its legality was as frankly admitted at the
North as at the South; it was, indeed, expressly
recognized in the Constitution of the United
States, and it was only one of a number of
differences which brought the two sections into
opposition, and finally precipitated a war.

The real cause of the antagonism of the two
sections at that day was the sectional rivalry
which existed between them. The Southern
States at first had a large excess of territory;
but when the first census was taken in 1790
there was but a small numerical excess over
the population of the North, and counting the
States about to be admitted, each section had
the same number of States.

In order to disarm jealousy growing out of
excess of area, and to facilitate the union, Virginia, the largest and most powerful State,

stripped herself of her vast northwestern territory and ceded to the general government that region from which, since then, have been carved the States of Ohio, Indiana, Illinois, Michigan, and a large part of Minnesota.

Then she gave her heart, Kentucky. These States, with one exception, were settled by a Northern population, and became Northern in sentiment, throwing a heavy preponderance into the Northern scale, and destroying the equilibrium which had existed, and upon which depended the peace and security of the nation.

From this time, the South was never permitted to increase her power without a corresponding increment to the North. Every step taken to restore the old equipoise was met and resisted as tending to Southern aggrandizement, and as a blow at the rights and privileges of the North. The purchase of the vast territory of Louisiana as early as 1803, and the admission of a State carved from the new acquisition, excited such violent opposition at the North that warnings came from New England threatening to dissolve the Union, which implied a view of the social compact not altogether consistent with that subsequently taken by New England statesmen. In 1812-15 New England, her trade being injured by the war with Great Britain, again threatened to secede. Not a great many years afterward, in 1819-20, the attempt to bring into the Union another portion of the vast Louisiana domain as the State of Missouri brought the struggle to a climax, and the existence of the Union was again seriously imperilled by the menace on the part of Northern States to dissolve it.

The difficulty was finally temporarily arranged by the noted Missouri Compromise, which admitted Missouri as a State, but prohibited slavery in all that portion of the Louisiana territory (except Missouri only) lying north of 36° 30′ north latitude.

It may be supposed that this philanthropic provision, which was effected by the Northern vote, was due to abhorrence of the peculiar institution which existed at the South. The histories we have been brought up on teach this. The fact is otherwise. Long subsequent to this, Abolitionists were held in equal contempt and encountered equal obloquy at the North and at the South.

The provision embraced in the Missouri Compromise was based on the facts that a considerable portion of the property of Southerners

357

consisted of slaves; that when the Southerner emigrated, he, like Abraham of old, carried his slaves with him; and that if he could not take them, he remained where he was. It was an effective means of preventing the extension of Southern influence. This was the first time that the sentiment against slavery was utilized as a lever to aid the North in its struggle for sectional supremacy. It was not destined to be the last time. It was found to be so potent a power that it was employed until eventually the Northern people came to believe themselves the chosen people of Israel and looked on the Southerners as the outcasts of the Gentiles.

It was in this controversy that the term "Secession" was first applied as indicating the action of a State in withdrawing from the Union.

In the light of subsequent events it is interesting to know that its use in this sense was due to a Northerner who threatened the South with a secession on the part of his people. This fixed intention on the part of the North to retain supremacy was manifested when Southern sagacity and statesmanship annexed the empire of Texas.

Again the North resisted this extension of

the Union even to the point of a threat to secede and destroy it. It was exhibited again upon the acquisition of California and New Mexico from Mexico. The line of the Missouri Compromise was extended West through the Texan territory, because Texas was Southern already, but when the Mexican domain was acquired, the North repudiated the principle of extension and claimed and took it all.

By these acts it was strong enough to maintain its supremacy in the government, and its power was exercised to establish a system of protection which fostered the manufacturers of the North and imposed the principal burden of taxation on the non-manufacturing South. Whilst the South governed the country, maintained her credit, extended her limits, fought her battles, and established her fame, the North secured protection and under its influences waxed fat.

Meantime the doctrine of abolition had flourished. In a generation it attained full growth. The sacred name of Liberty inspires the human heart.

The propagandists of abolition appealed not to the Northern people, but to Christendom, and the South stood at once with the forces of the world arrayed against her. Her every act was misjudged, her every word was misinterpreted.

She met this censure with sublime scorn. Arraigned at the judgment bar, she hurled defiance at her judges.

She devoted all her intellectual resources. and they were immense, to polemical warfare. In her intemperate anger she permitted herself to abandon her point of vantage. She exercised her constitutional privilege and seceded. A great sentiment for the Union suddenly thrilled the North. It declared war. The result is known.

It is to this section, heretofore inherently incapable of comprehending her, that the South has left the writing of the history of her civilization. It may appear to be not a matter of importance who writes the story of this country. Manifestly the South has so regarded it. It is, however, a sad fallacy.

The writings of the propagandists of the North destroyed the power of the South and brought her to destruction.

And now unless we look to it we shall go down to posterity as a blot on our time, and a reproach to American civilization.

Does this seem to you a small thing? In it lies the difference between fame and infamy, between corruption and immortality.

Does it appear to you impossible? Do we not now stand at the bar of history, charged with the crime of attempting to perpetuate human slavery, and for this purpose with conspiracy to destroy the best government the world has ever seen—the American Union?

We do stand so charged, and if we refuse to make our defence, the judgment of history will be against us for all time.

Before fifty years shall have passed, unless we look to it, the South's action will have gone into history as the defence of human slavery, and it will be deemed the world over to have been as great a crime against nature as the slave trade itself.

How may this be avoided? By establishing the fact that it was not the South, but the time, which was responsible for slavery; and that this slavery with all its evils, and they were many, was the only civilizer that the African has yet known. By recording ere it be too late the true history of the South; by preserving and transmitting the real life of that civilization, so that future ages may know not what its enemies thought it to be, but what it in truth was.

Up to the present more than half of the material for a history of this nation has been overlooked—the material contained in the life of the Southern people. The history that has been written is as an ancient palimpsest, in which the writing that is read is but a monkish legend, whilst underneath, unnoticed and effaced, lies the record of eternal truth.

It remains now to suggest a few elements of the material from which the only true history of the South and of this nation is to be constructed.

One of the chief elements of strength in the old civilization of the South was self-respect. Arrogant, as it is charged to have been, and as it may have been, pride lifted it above all meanness and elevated it into the realm of greatness. Its standard was so high that contemplation of it made men upright, and aspiration to it made them noble. I belong to the new order of Southern life. I am one of those who can feel the thrill of new energies fill my heart; I think I can see and admit the incalculable waste, the narrow limitations of the old. I give my loyal and enthusiastic adherence to the

present, with all its fresh and glorious possibilities; but I shall never forget that it is to
the Old South that the New South owes all that
is best and noblest in its being.

Can we ever secure the respect of the world
if we have no self-respect?

Reverence for the greatness of its past, pride
of race, are two cardinal elements in national
strength.

They made the Greek; they made the Roman;
they made the Saxon; they made the Southerner.

We are the inheritors of a thousand years
of courage and of devotion to principle. And
without these two things we should deserve the
contempt of mankind and the reprobation of
God.

Contemporary history is being recorded by
writers organically disabled to comprehend
the action of the South. It rests with the South
whether she shall go down to posterity as they
have pictured her—the breeder of tyrants, the
defender of slavery, the fomenter of treason.

Scripta ferunt annos.

We are not a race to pass and leave no memorial on our time. We live with more than
Grecian energy. We must either leave our his-

tory to be written by those who do not understand it, or we must write it ourselves.

If we are willing to be handed down to coming time as a race of slave-drivers and traitors, it is as well to continue in our state of lethargy and acquiescence; but if we retain the instincts of men, and desire to transmit to our children the untarnished name and spotless fame which our forefathers bequeathed to us, we must awake to the exigencies of the matter. We stand charged at the judgment bar of history with these crimes. It is useless to close our eyes to the fact. We stand so indicted, and posterity is the tribunal that shall try us. If we refuse to plead, the opportunity will pass away, the verdict of time will be ''guilty,'' and the punishment will be the *peine forte et dure*. To leave us perpetually bound under the burden of guilt which some would bind on our shoulders, would be to withdraw from the divine heritage of patriotism the best soil for its growth on this continent; to debar from its influences the best material for war that the Anglo-American race has produced.

Whatever else may be said, of this much are we sure, that the South and its civilization produced a race of soldiers which has never been surpassed. Present history may multiply her numbers and magnify her resources, but the original archives show with a conclusiveness which cannot be withstood, the splendid heroism of the fight which, under the inspiration of what she deemed a sacred cause, she made, not against the Union, but against the world.

It was not for interest that she fought; for war was not to her interest. It was not to dissolve the Union that she seceded; for secession was again and again rejected by the border States. It was only when war was declared and the Constitution was set aside that these States, driven to their last resort, and, by Mr. Lincoln's call for troops, forced to take the one side or the other, to secede or to invade their sister States, exercised their constitutional rights and withdrew from the Union.

A proof of the deep sincerity of their principles is the unanimity with which the South accepted the issue. From the moment that war was declared, the whole people were in arms. It was not merely the secessionist who enlisted, but the stanch Union man; not simply the slaveholder, but the mountaineer; the poor white fought as valorously as the great land-owner; the women fought as well as the men; for, whilst the men were in the field the women and children at home waited and starved without a murmur and without a doubt.

Some years ago I was shown a worn and faded letter written on old Confederate paper with pale Confederate ink. It had been taken from the breast-pocket of a dead private soldier of a Georgia regiment after one of the battles around Richmond. It was from his sweetheart. They were plain and illiterate people, for it was badly written and badly spelled. In it she told him that she loved him; that she had always loved him since they had gone to school together, in the little log schoolhouse in the woods; that she was sorry she had always treated him so badly, and that now, if he would get a furlough and come home, she would marry him.

Then, as if fearful that this temptation might prove too strong to be resisted, there was a little postscript scrawled across the blue Confederate paper: "Don't come without a furlough, for if you don't come honorable, I won't marry you."

Was this the spirit of rebellion? A whole people was in arms. A nation had arisen. It was the apotheosis of a race.

When Varro lost the battle of Cannæ, where

THE WANT OF A HISTORY

the flower of the Roman knighthood was cut down, the Roman Senate voted thanks to the consul *quod de republica non desperasset;* when Lee, with tattered standards and broken battalions, recrossed the Potomac, after Gettysburg, the South exhibited greater devotion to him than when he forced Burnside staggering back across the Rappahannock. When he abandoned Richmond and started on his march Southward, the South still trusted him as implicitly as when, with consummate generalship and a loss to the enemy of more than his own entire army, he had at Spottsylvania wedged Grant from his prey.

That last retreat surpasses in heroism the retreat of the Ten Thousand. There was but a handful left of the army of Northern Virginia. The attrition of four years of war had worn away the heroic army. Starvation had destroyed a part of what the sword had left, and had shrunken the forms of the small remnant; but the glorious courage, the indomitable spirit of the Southern soldiery gleamed forth; and it had no more thought of surrender then than when it had first burst into flame on the victorious field of Bull Run. It was the crystallization of Southern courage.

Across the desolated land it retired like a

wounded lion, sore pressed by unnumbered
foes—stopping only to fight, for there was no
rest nor food, until at last on that fateful morning it found the horizon filled with steel. It
was hemmed in by the enemy, by the best
equipped army that has stood on American soil,
led by one of the greatest generals, the magnani-
mous Grant, and the Southern general saw that
resistance was annihilation. Even in that hour
of its extremity, the one cry of the little band
to the adored Lee was to be led against them
once more.

The chronicler, who can see in this only the
perverseness of rebellion, lacks the essential
spirit of the historian. The politician who can
discuss it with derision or can view it with
indifference will never rise to the plane of statesmanship.

The deliberate and persistent endeavor to
hold in contempt the people that could produce
so sublime a spectacle and to forbid them par-
ticipation in the Union, is a greater wrong to
the Nation than was secession. It is an attempt
to keep alienated from the Union a race that
has ever hated with fervor but loved with passion; of a race that withdrew from the Union
under a belief in a principle so sincere, so deep,

that it was almost idolatrous; of a race that has now under new conditions turned to the Union all the devotion which under different teaching and conditions was once given to the several States; devotion which when directed against the Union shook it to its foundation, and now is destined to guard it and preserve it throughout its existence.

The history of the South is yet to be written. He who writes it need not fear for his reward. Such a one must have at once the instinct of the historian and the wisdom of the philosopher. He must possess the talisman that shall discover truth amid all the heaps of falsehood, though they were piled upon it like Pelion on Ossa. He must have the sagacity to detect whatever of evil existed in the civilization he shall chronicle, though it be gleaming with the gilding of romance; he must have the fortitude to resist all temptation to deflect by so much as a hair's breadth from the absolute and the inexorable facts, even if an angel should attempt to beguile him. He must know and tell the truth, the whole truth, and nothing but the truth, so help him, God!

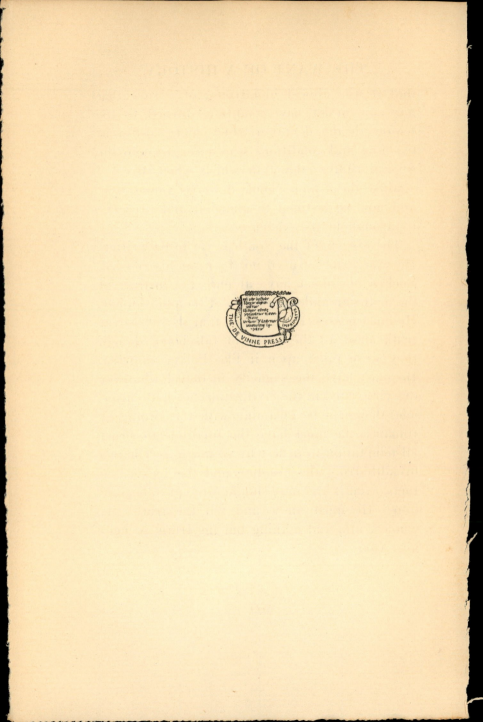